HOW TO FACILITATE

PRODUCTIVE
PROJECT PLANNING
MEETINGS

HOW TO FACILITATE
PRODUCTIVE PROJECT PLANNING MEETINGS

A PRACTICAL GUIDE TO ENSURING PROJECT SUCCESS

RICH MALTZMAN | JIM STEWART

MAVEN HOUSE

Published by Maven House Press, 4 Snead Ct., Palmyra, VA 22963; 610.883.7988; www.mavenhousepress.com.

Special discounts on bulk quantities of Maven House Press books are available to corporations, professional associations, and other organizations. For details contact the publisher.

While this publication is designed to provide accurate and authoritative information in regard to the subject matter covered, it is sold with the understanding that the publisher is not engaged in rendering legal, accounting, or other professional service. If legal advice or other expert assistance is required, the services of a competent professional person should be sought. — From the Declaration of Principles jointly adopted by a Committee of the American Bar Association and a Committee of Publishers and Associations

"PMI," "PMP," and "PMBOK" are registered marks of the Project Management Institute, Inc.

Library of Congress Control Number: 2018948896

Paperback ISBN: 978-1-938548-26-0

Printed in the United States of America.

CONTENTS

LIST OF EXHIBITS

LIST OF EXHIBITS

FOREWORD

Harold Kerzner, PhD

Too many companies are plagued with meeting mania – project managers (and their team members) go from meeting to meeting each day with very little being accomplished. Meeting mania is a costly curse. Assume that you're managing a one-year project that requires the project manager to attend ten meetings a month. If each meeting has fifteen participants in attendance and lasts for two hours, and a fully loaded hourly labor rate is $200, then the yearly meeting costs for this project will exceed $700,000. If the company is working on fifty projects concurrently, the yearly meeting cost for all projects will exceed $35 million!!! Effective project planning meetings can significantly reduce this amount.

Meetings are conducted to share information, report performance, and make decisions. When I was a young project manager a few decades ago, I attended my first project planning meeting. The outcome of the meeting were two words that would bring fear to my heart for years to come: *action items*. I couldn't understand why many of my meetings resulted in *action items* rather than *decisions*. The problem, I soon discovered, was that the planning meeting required decisions on how resources would be committed and assigned, but many of the participants in attendance were not authorized by their functional managers to make such decisions without their managers' concurrence.

Having recognized the trap I was in, I then asked each team member, prior to the start of the planning meetings, whether they were authorized to make planning and resource commitment decisions for their functional groups. If they were not authorized, then their functional managers would be invited to attend the planning meetings, or I'd ask them to attain their managers' delegation. Some functional managers began asking when during the meeting their involvement would be essential, because they didn't want to attend a two-hour meeting where only fifteen minutes would involve their functional area. Therefore, to circumvent this problem, I prepared a detailed planning meeting agenda, which made it easier for functional managers to know exactly which timeslot they should attend. This made it easier to get functional involvement in a timely manner.

While meeting agendas and knowing which team members possessed decision-making authority for their functional areas had reduced some of my meeting mania, there was still the issue of action items, which involved customer involvement and customer decision-making. Planning meetings that involve customers are significantly costlier than internal planning meetings because of travel time, airfare, meals, and lodgings. Most of the meetings with the clients involved handouts as discussion points. Giving the client a copy of the handouts at the beginning of the planning meeting, and then expecting them to understand everything rapidly and be prepared to make an on-the-spot decision, is unrealistic. This created more action items and quite often more travel costs than budgeted for. The solution was to send the client a copy of the handouts at least a week before the meeting. This allowed them to digest the material and be prepared to make decisions.

The twists and turns of today's virtual world present an additional threat (and opportunity) for project planning meetings. In this environment, it helps to have some guidelines and to benefit from the experience of those who have mastered that particular aspect of project planning meetings.

Whether in person, virtual, or hybrid, project planning meetings set the stage for most of the other meetings that will occur on your projects. If you wish to reduce meeting mania and action items, then the starting point must be your planning meetings. This book should therefore be a must-read for all project managers who wish to set themselves up for successful meetings from the beginning of the project.

PREFACE

WE *KNOW YOU NEED THIS BOOK*. How could we possibly know that? We haven't spied on you or read your emails, although they were indeed offered to us by a certain operative whom we are not at liberty to name at the current time. But that's the subject for a different book. Between us, we've been to 14,829 meetings and led 358 of them (disclaimer: the numbers are approximate). In any case, we've been to a lot of meetings – project planning meetings in particular – and have led hundreds of them. They don't all go well, and yet they are fundamental to project success because meetings are the most important components of the most important element of a project manager's job – communications. We want to share our experience with you. And we want to share the experience of experts we've pulled together to help us provide the very best and very latest advice about running a productive project planning meeting.

We've made some assumptions about your knowledge of basic project management principles and vocabulary. However, if you need a refresher, we've got you covered. See our Refresher appendix first if you want to be sure you're up to speed.

How to Read This Book

We believe that in order to get the most value from this book, it would be wise to read it cover to cover prior to planning your meeting. We say this because, while the core of the book does contain the nuts and bolts of running the meeting, a significant portion of it deals with important framing and contextual background such as team building, working with different cultures, virtual sessions, and, yes, even war stories. Taken holistically, all of these factors should help you be much better prepared for what should then be one of the most productive, forward-thinking meetings you've ever had.

ACKNOWLEDGEMENTS

Eileen Dowse PhD, Chair of INIFAC
Harold Kerzner, PhD
Wayne Turmel
Teresa Lawrence
Janice Preston
Steve Martin
Richard D. Lewis
Menno Valkenberg
War Story Contributors

CHAPTER ONE

The Status of Projects Today

B OOK AFTER PROJECT MANAGEMENT BOOK, report after project management report, study after project management study show that
projects are not much more successful today than they were decades ago
– of course, depending somewhat on one's measure of success. One thing
that's also been a common thread in books, reports, and studies is that
better planning is one of the key differentiating factors.

Allan Zucker (2016) has summarized the fairly depressing results
of 20+ years of project success from The Standish Group's CHAOS Report surveys. The data show that, generally, there has been no change in
project success rates since 1994 (see Exhibit 1.1). Digging deeper, Zucker
found some of the elements that had driven higher success rates, offering some rays of hope in these decades' worth of flat and drab results.
Amongst those rays of hope, he says that "teams that can effectively communicate and collaborate are better at resolving issues and solving problems."

As you will see in the following chapter, there is evidence that planning is important to project success, and it's clear that meetings are needed for that planning to take place. After all, few projects have only one
team member.

The Project Management Institute's *A Guide to the Project Management Body of Knowledge (PMBOK® Guide) – Sixth Edition* details forty

1

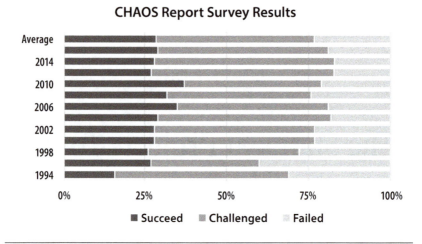

CHAOS Report Survey Results

Exhibit 1.1. Standish Group's CHAOS reports show little change in project success over the years.

nine processes that should be performed to run a successful project. Almost half – twenty four – are planning processes. Clearly PMI is sending a message. As carpenters are fond of saying, measure twice, cut once.

This book focuses on planning – the very down-to-earth, gritty part of planning: project planning meetings. However, it also deals with more "mundane" meetings such as status and lessons learned sessions.

Whether the meeting is taking place in room 201A, just down the hall and on the left, on video screens worldwide, or in some combination of the nearby and the virtual, the project planning meeting is a staple of a project manager's world. And if you agree that they're fundamental to project success, and that planning is key to the success of projects, well, you get the idea: improved planning meetings mean better project results.

Our main focus is on the project kickoff meeting, but we'll cover project planning meetings in general and provide experience-based tips to help you facilitate effective, productive, interesting, and even fun project planning meetings.

CHAPTER TWO

The Importance of Planning

Plans are worthless, but planning is everything.

— Dwight D. Eisenhower

S INCE PLANNING IS EVERYTHING, we want to dedicate a proper portion of coverage to this topic and make sure that you have the motivation and tools to do it right.

> NOTE – Many people colloquially refer to a timeline or schedule as a plan. For this book, we will refer to a timeline as a schedule and any document that facilitates planning as a plan. The former is typically manifested in a Gantt chart or network diagram; the latter in a document or documents.

Planning is Dynamic

We begin by asserting the difference between a *plan* and *planning*. We are discussing the importance of planning. What may appear to be a trivial difference is actually quite significant, as best expressed by Jack Duggan (2012) in his paper, "Managing the DANCE: Think Design, Not Plan."

The DANCE to which Duggan refers is an acronym for Dynamic and changing, Ambiguous and uncertain, Non-linear and unpredictable,

Complex, and Emergent – this is the nature of projects today. So having a plan (the noun) means that you have created something static. By shifting to the gerund form – *planning* – we take into account that the plan will need to evolve.

Project planning is indeed an ongoing process, whether the methodology is waterfall or agile. (We'll define those terms later.) And as projects DANCE more now than ever before, that means planning is more important now than ever before.

Planning Makes a Difference

Andy Crowe's book, *Alpha Project Managers: What The Top 2% Know That Everyone Else Does Not* (2016), summarizes a landmark survey of over 800 project managers to find out what the top two percent (the Alphas) do that other project managers do not. A key finding: *Alpha project managers spent twice as much time in the planning phase of their projects than did non-alphas.*

Does planning make a difference? Yes, significantly. In his paper, "The Importance of the Planning Phase to Project Success," author Pedro Serrador (2012) wrote about the correlation of project success with the effort put forth up front (and ongoing) in planning projects. Amongst his conclusions:

- Pressure exists in the project environment to reduce the time spent planning rather than increase it.
- The level of planning completeness is positively correlated with project success in the construction industry.
- Planning is associated with project success, both project efficiency and overall project success.

So although there will be pressure to do without planning, you should be looking at the compelling reasons to achieve what Serrador calls "planning completeness." This will, in turn require project planning meetings. That brings us to the importance of the meetings themselves and the compelling need to do them right or not at all.

CHAPTER THREE

The Importance of Meetings

Pick any major event, trip, or undertaking in your life and think about the time, energy, and work put into making sure everything went off without a hitch. Then think about the stress and aggravation you experienced those times when things didn't go as planned. Doesn't your project warrant at least as much planning as, say, your upcoming vacation to the Netherlands to catch the cheese festival in Alkmaar?

As a discipline, project management for usiness projects works the same way as for vacation projects, except on a greater scale and involving more stakeholders and a larger pool of resources. It can include external vendors, several other internal and intra-departmental team members (as well as their schedules and input), additional parameters such as cost, quality, timing, constant coordination and communication, and associated risks.

Without planning, projects suffer from:

- Lack of strategic alignment
- Cost, quality, and time-constraint issues and scope creep
- Lack of stakeholder commitment and resources
- Inefficient use of resources
- Frustration and morale issues amongst team members

◆ Communication issues

◆ Increased risk

In chapter 7, we refer to a case study about Karyn Salas, fictional Mayor of Escondido, California, and her project to build a home based on principles of sustainability. She'll be wanting to kick off her project with excellent planning – her home, and her political future, depend on it. Take a moment to read the case study so you'll have that story in your mind as you read through the book – it will help pull things together for you.

CHAPTER FOUR

The Status of Meetings Today

IN A *FORBES* ARTICLE, "Why Most Meetings are Awful and What You Can Do About It," Author Erika Andersen (2014) says:

> I hate bad meetings. It's partly due to my fundamental impatience and partly to my experience of how productive and even fun a good meeting can be. Fortunately for me, I'm seldom [the victim of] lousy meetings: I'm generally either facilitating (in which case I better be able to make it useful, or why are you paying me), or it's a meeting in my own company (and if I can't keep those from being bad, yikes.)

She identifies three main reasons why meetings are awful:

1. **We don't clarify the *who*.** In a bad meeting, most of the attendees are sitting there wondering what's in it for them . . . and generally concluding that the answer is "not much." Poor meetings generally consist of somebody talking and everyone else pretending to listen, or a conversation that only involves a couple of the people present.

2. **We don't clarify the *why*.** Recently a friend of mine regaled me a with a tale of a particularly awful meeting he'd been required to attend. He said, "The worst thing about it was that no one really

THE
UGLY TRUTH
ABOUT
MEETINGS

MEETINGS ARE MEANT TO BE AN ENGINE OF PRODUCTIVITY IN THE WORKPLACE.

But, what's meant to be an efficient way for people to get together to discuss ideas, debate issues, overcome obstacles and drive outcomes, often doesn't turn out like that at all. The truth is that many meetings end up being about as valuable as a Snapchat post -- people talk, the ideas quickly disappear into the ether with no outcomes or follow up.

Exhibit 4.1. The Ugly Truth About Meetings: Meetings often don't improve productivity in the workplace. Courtesy of Fuze.com.

knew why we were there, what the meeting was supposed to be about, or what was expected of us. Beyond a superficial 'We're meeting about our 2013 goals' memo that went out beforehand, we had zero useful information. And it didn't get any better . . .

WHAT'S THE HARM IN UNPRODUCTIVE MEETINGS?

▶ **IT WASTES MONEY:**

More than $37 **BILLION** per year is spent on unproductive meetings.

▶ **IT WASTES TIME:**

There are **25 MILLION** meetings per day in the U.S.

▶ **IT WASTES YOUR ORGANIZATION'S TIME:**

15% of an organization's **COLLECTIVE TIME** is spent in meetings, a percentage that has increased every year since 2008.

Middle managers spend **35% OF THEIR TIME** in meetings.

Upper management spends **50% OF THEIR TIME** in meetings.

People spend up to **4 HOURS PER WEEK** preparing for status update meetings.

YOU SPEND ALL THAT TIME AND MONEY BUT...

Most meetings are **UNPRODUCTIVE.**

In fact, executives consider more than **67%** of meetings to be failures.

Exhibit 4.1 (cont.). Meetings can waste money, your time, and your organizations time.

I left not knowing any more about the purpose of the meeting than when I walked in."

3. **We don't clarify the *what's next*.** Even if you have a good meeting, one that feels focused and productive, if nothing happens afterwards . . . it's a still a bad meeting. If the next steps after a

WHAT'S CAUSING UNPRODUCTIVE MEETINGS?

1. MULTITASKING

92% of survey respondents confessed to multitasking during meetings

69% admitted to checking email

41% admitted to multitasking "often" or "all the time"

49% admitted to doing other, unrelated work

2. REMOTE PARTICIPANTS AREN'T ENGAGED

It can be hard for remote participants to follow along, stay engaged and feel like they can contribute.

In fact, **80%** of messages we receive come from **BODY LANGUAGE**

– something that is hard to pick up on when you're on the phone.

BLAH BLAH BLAH

3. LACK OF PLANNING AND STRUCTURE

Facilitating effective meetings is a skill that can be learned and honed. Considering the amount of time we spend in meetings, more companies should invest in improving meeting effectiveness.

Exhibit 4.1 (cont.). Meetings are often unproductive because of lack of meeting planning and structure and participants multitasking and not engaged.

meeting aren't clear or simply don't happen, people will experience the meeting as a kind of bait-and-switch . . . good while it lasted, but ultimately useless. And if you're the responsible party, you'll lose credibility. Clear, tangible outcomes from a meeting you run aren't just a nice-to-do, they're an important signal to others that you're competent and trustworthy.

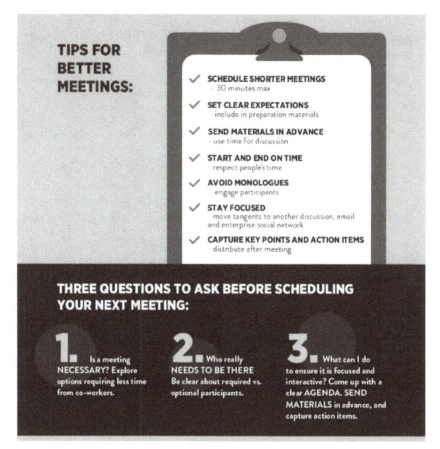

Exhibit 4.1 (cont.). Three things can improve meetings – making sure the meeting is necessary, the people who need to be there are there, and a clear agenda is sent to participants in advance of the meeting.

In his article, "Meetings Suck, Make Them Better," Tom Searcy (2012) provides several tips to remedy the three problems:

1. **Think short.** Create and advertise a tight agenda with clear outcomes.

2. **Collaborate.** If you want engagement, you need to orchestrate it. Build questions and discussions right into the agenda.

3. **Use the ensemble cast.** You (may) need multiple presenters on your team for a larger meeting.

4. **Follow up.** Don't promise to follow up if you're not going to do so, and quickly.

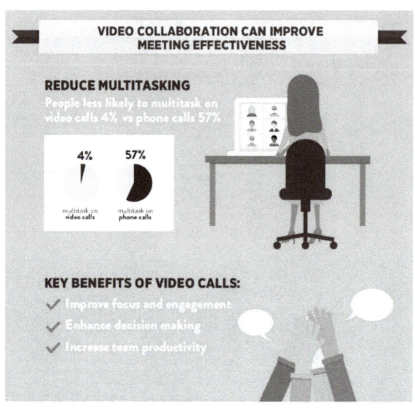

Exhibit 4.1 (cont.). For virtual meetings, video calls are more beneficial than phone calls.

"Hold a meeting and make attendance optional. Then,
you'll know who REALLY wants to be there."

— *Daniel Mezick, agile coach*

(We don't necessarily endorse this, but it's an interesting philosophy.)

CHARACTERISTICS OF POOR MEETINGS	
The Meeting	Project Management Root Cause
Meeting purpose is unclear.	Project's purpose is unclear or unpopular, or the project manager hasn't done a good job of setting an agenda.
The right people aren't expressing their thoughts.	Project manager hasn't set proper ground rules for team behavior and/or some people are uncomfortable speaking up.
The wrong people are invited, or people are missing.	Proper project stakeholder population hasn't been identified, or the project manager hasn't made a compelling case for attendance.
Inadequate time has been allocated for the meeting.	Project priorities (the order of constraints) haven't been properly determined, or the project manager has allowed someone to hijack the meeting.
The agenda is poorly designed (or there's no agenda).	Project's communication management plan is absent or lacking, or the project manager is ineffective at planning meetings.
The meeting facility is unsuitable (noise/capacity).	

Exhibit 4.2. The causes of poor meetings are well understood.

Are Poor Meetings a Symptom or a Cause?

When was the last time that you just *could not wait* to get to a meeting? Not to leave, but to get *to* it. Do you recall counting the days, hours, minutes, seconds until that meeting finally started? Probably not. The reason? The meetings weren't designed well. And this can spell trouble, not only for the meeting, but for the project (and by extension, the organization). In fact, it may be the other way around. Perhaps the poor meetings are a symptom of something larger, in addition to (or even instead of) being the cause of trouble for the project. And then, some people just simply do not like meetings. Hopefully you can be part of the solution for poor meetings – and turn that around for them.

In Exhibit 4.2 we've summarized some characteristics of poor meetings and, separately, the possible causes of these characteristics.

Ask yourself: Besides really great snacks, what entices you to attend a meeting (as a team member, not as the project manager)?

◆   You want to contribute.

◆   You want to make sure a key point is made.

◆   You want to express a creative idea.

◆   You enjoy the social aspect.

◆   You want to be updated on the project's progress.

◆   You are intensely invested in the outcome of the project.

As the meeting planner, think about these enticements. If you understand the team's motivation for attending, and what will make them get the most out of the meeting, you'll be able to get more productive (and enjoyable) use of the team participants.

> "Because there's consequences for what we do . . .
> Consequences for me and you."
>
> — *Robert Cray, bluesman*

Understanding the Consequences

Whether effect or cause, if a meeting fails to meet its objectives, there are consequences.

Exhibit 4.3 shows some effects (consequences) of poor meetings.

Note that these consequences of meeting ineffectiveness yield the exact opposite of typical critical success factors (CSFs) for projects. Our Glossary appendix has an example showing the linkage between objectives and CSFs. For now, know that a CSF describes the way in which you will get to the objective – the means to the end.

CONSEQUENCES OF POOR MEETINGS	
Consequences for the Meeting	Consequences for the Project
Project is disconnected from the mission/vision of the organization.	Project management is a success, but the project is a failure.
Scope is incomplete.	Project doesn't deliver what was promised or delivers what the project manager *thought* was promised.
Team members are undervalued or feel that their opinions don't count.	Potentially critical Subject Matter Expert (SME) input is lost and team members are alienated.
Team member feels that the meeting didn't go well.*	Establish precedent for poor communications and team dynamics for the remainder of the project.
People are confused.	People are alienated, some leaving the project.
Some risks are unidentified.	No risk response plan results in the use of much duct tape and WD-40 (or the equivalent adhesives and lubricants).
Conflicts and arguments occur at the meeting.	Downside: If they're personal alienation will likely occur, and people may leave the team or only provide "sarcastic compliance."
	Upside: If the conflict is "tamed" and handled so that it's focused on issues, conflict can drive creativity and passion.
Meeting is argumentative and combative.	Team members depart or shut down.

Exhibit 4.3. If a meeting fails to meet its objectives there are consequences.
* Every company seems to have someone whose job it is to go to a meeting, fold their arms, and say, "It won't work, it just won't work." Then they go home at night and proudly tell their spouse how many projects they screwed up that day.

CHAPTER FIVE

General Tips for Successful Meetings

G IVEN THE FACT THAT MANY COMPANIES TODAY ARE MULTINATIONAL, it's not at all uncommon to work with people from different cultures. We both work on a regular basis with people from India, China, and Finland, to name just a few. (We'll be talking later in the book about working with different cultures.)

Since this book is about meetings, we thought it would be interesting to consider a chart that details how long it takes to start a meeting in various cultures. While there are some humorous elements to it, by and large it has been confirmed to us, not only by our own experience but also by that of our students, that, yes, Germans start meetings right on time, and Latin countries tend to be more laid-back about starting times.

Lesson learned? Account for differences. If you're an American holding a meeting in America, visitors should understand that you'll be starting on time. But if you're an American working in, say, France, well, just relax and go with the flow (see Exhibit 5.1).

Be Sensory – Not Sen-sorry

Since planning meetings are so important, and since communication and collaboration (the guts of any meeting) are a way to improve upon the lackluster success rate of projects, you can sense the importance of

Cultural Difference in Meetings

GERMANY		Formal introduction. Sit down. Begin.
FINLAND		Formal introduction. Cup of coffee. Sit down. Begin.
U.S.		Informal introduction. Cup of coffee. Wisecrack. Begin.
U.K.		Formal introduction. Cup of tea and biscuits. 10 mins. small talk (weather, comfort, sport). Casual beginning.
FRANCE		Formal introduction. 15 mins. small talk (politics, scandal, etc.). Begin.
JAPAN		Formal introduction. Protocol seating. Green tea. 15–20 mins. small talk (harmonious pleasantries). Sudden signal from senior Japanese. Begin.
SPAIN/ ITALY		10–30 min. small talk (soccer, family matters) while others arrive. Begin when all are there.

```
0      5      10     15     20     25     30
```

Exhibit 5.1. You should account for cultural differences when structuring meetings. ©2010 Richard D. Lewis, Richard Lewis Communications Ltd., www.crossculture.com.

holding planning meetings. In fact, let's dwell on our *senses* for a moment. All of them. We like to say, "Be sensory – not sen-sorry." We encourage you to use your senses of sight, sound, taste, touch, and smell to help drive successful planning meetings for your project.

We've taken some liberty with the words describing our senses here – using more expanded, colloquial definitions. Now, don't be too sensitive about that!

See the Light

Your project has been chartered – or so we assume – at this point. So you know what the prize – the end-result – should look like. Now you not only need to keep your eyes on the prize, you need to keep your *team's* eyes on the prize – the proverbial light at the end of the tunnel. This means that during planning you should be constantly refining the project's objectives. If your project has a visual outcome (such as a new hospital wing, a bridge, even a book or software application) keep an image of the finished project product in sight of the team as much as possible. This is the light at the end of the tunnel. So don't let your team work in the dark. Light the way with whatever it is that your project will provide the organization.

Keep in Touch

We use the expression "keep in touch" to remind you, as a planner, that the planning process can only be successful if all who contribute or care about the project know its appropriate details – ground rules, expectations, methods, tools. In fact, we have always asserted that in any email communication, particularly meeting announcements and notes from meetings, the distribution list is almost as important as the content.

Even the notification method you use for the meeting may need to vary depending on your audience. For example, some people will want (or need) a voice message or text in addition to an email invitation. The right people (and only the right people) should know about the meeting, the purpose of the meeting, the expectations of the meeting outcome, and, especially, any actions for them that come from the meeting. Over-communication is not necessarily a bad thing.

One good question to ask at the start of a series of planning meetings is: "Have we got the right people here?" It's like that old teacher's joke, "If you're not present, please raise your hand," except that this time it's serious. If your attendees know of colleagues who should be at the meeting, that's critical information for you as the project manager. So be sure your meeting is reaching out and touching everyone it should.

No Accounting for Taste

Here we use the word *taste* in the sense of "there's no accounting for taste." In other words, it's a reference to choices of style, fashion, even of significant others – *that* sort of taste. This can serve as a reminder that:

- There's often more than one style of planning.
- Your team will have their own tastes when it comes to how they're involved in planning, meeting styles, communication styles. Seek input from them in advance of the meeting for such

preferences. Listen to these views, and consider them all in your decisions, but remember, as the project manager, you're in charge and you make these decisions.

◆ Your team may have a variety of preferences when it comes to distributing planning information. (See "Keep in Touch" above)

◆ People are not inside your head. Don't assume that they all think like you or share the same enthusiasm that you do for your project. As likely as not, they have several other projects and this is, for them, just one more obligation.

The Sweet Smell of Success

Sense of smell, like that of a hound dog, is the ability to sniff out threats and opportunities. We need a complete capture of two things in particular at the early planning stages:

◆ Stakeholders

◆ Risks

It's imperative that these be fully sniffed out so that your lists of stakeholders and risks are complete.

Your failure to identify a stakeholder means that all of the value this stakeholder could provide is absent – or that the dangers that may come with this stakeholder won't be considered. For example, if your construction company has access to a regulatory expert who knows the details of permitting and the legal aspects of your type of construction, we strongly recommend that you include them as a stakeholder or you'll lose important intelligence that could stop or significantly delay your project.

A risk (threat or opportunity) that hasn't been sniffed out represents a missed opportunity to exploit, or a threat that you must now deal with as a workaround.

A brief digression on the importance of stakeholders

Let's first define what a stakeholder is: *Any individual, group, or organization that can affect, be affected by, or perceive itself to be affected by an initiative (program, project, activity, or risk).*

So what does that mean for us? Quite simply, it means that stakeholders are people who have a *stake* in the project – it affects them in some way. So it's your job to ferret out who the stakeholders are (your sponsor can help), find out what their expectations are, and keep them engaged throughout the life of the project.

What happens when you keep the stakeholders in the dark? Here's an example close to home for both of us. A few years ago, the city of Boston opted to try to bring the Olympics to town. The people in charge of providing the bid to the International Olympic Committee advised them that the Harvard University swimming pool could be used for the swimming events, and an area known as Widett Circle could be used as the Olympic Village. Both great ideas! Except for two things: First, *nobody told Harvard that that was the plan.* And second, *Widett Circle?* Must be some empty lot, right? Nope, it's an area just south of Route 93 where the local purveyors of seafood sell their wares to restaurants. In both cases those stakeholders – because that's what they were – said no, thank you. That isn't the entire reason this bid collapsed, but it was a main contributor.

Want your project to collapse in an unceremonious heap? Keep your stakeholders in the dark and surprise them.

Hear Ye, Hear Ye . . .

The expression "having your ear to the ground" probably originated from Native Americans who used the technique to detect movement of animals or people from a distance. It means that it's helpful to be well-aware of trends, opinions, even rumors. The way any project manager can do this is to use MBWA (Management By Walking Around). Be aware of the latest news about your project and the project team (even on a personal level). Who just had a child or grandchild? Did someone have a skiing accident and will be out for a few weeks? These details, along with (of course) being up-to-date on actual, technical project news, is key. Make your meetings relevant by including newsy, pertinent information and assure that it's appropriately shared. In particular, make sure you're hearing the lessons learned from past project managers who have preceded you on similar projects.

Synthesizing the Sensory Information

Now that you've gathered all of this sensory information, it's up to your command center (the brain!) to synthesize and organize it into knowledge. You'll use your information and your project management know-how to determine, for example, how you'll:

- Identify, analyze, and respond to risk.

- Identify, engage with, and manage stakeholders.

- Acquire resources.

- Communicate.

- Lead and develop the team.

- Set and manage scope.

- Determine and baseline the schedule and budget.

Be sure you customize this list for your projects. In many cases, the answers will come from planning meetings. This book provides resources and templates to help you with all of the above.

What is a Successful Project Meeting?

According to Marieke Strobbe et al. in their book *Five Frustrations of Project Managers* (2017), "An effective project meeting sees participants leave with fresh insights and energy, generated through confidence in the direction of the project and each other." In fact, their book has an entire chapter dedicated to project meetings – it's one of the "five frustrations." They see a project planning meeting as a microprocess of the project – a "fundamental moment for team collaboration." However, as the authors note, it can become a source of irritation if agenda items aren't covered, urgent (but not necessarily important) items draw attention from key non-urgent concerns, and/or the meetings become boring, tedious, and irresolute.

This is where planning and meetings intersect – in the form of planning *for* meetings. "A lack of focus on preparation can lead to the meeting itself costing a lot of time and being characterized by negative energy. In our experience a greater focus on preparation than on execution improves the quality and results of [project] meetings." (See Exhibit 5.2)

We've adapted several of their suggestions for successful meetings:

- Spend time preparing and evaluating meetings so that you can make them effective in advance (not in a real-time, reactionary mode).

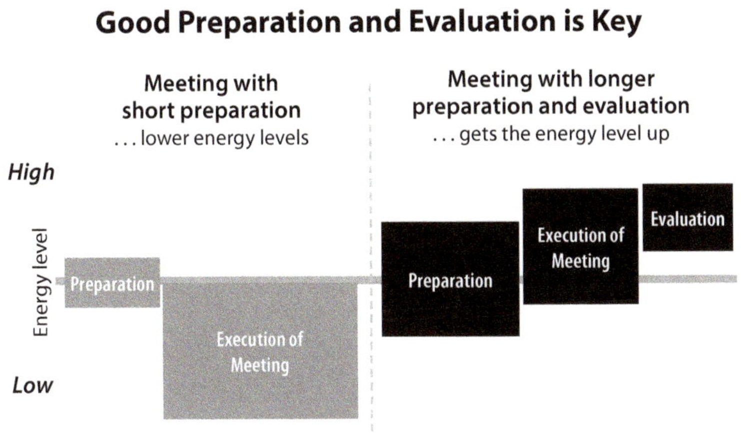

Good Preparation and Evaluation is Key

Exhibit 5.2. Preparation for the meeting, and evaluation of the meeting after it's over, is key to having successful meetings. From *Five Frustrations of Project Managers* (**Strobbe 2017**).

- ◆ Ensure that you're aware of the energy level of the meeting attendees and adjust accordingly (frequent breaks, amount of animation needed).

- ◆ Decide on your own role: are *you* the facilitator? This is a natural role for the project manager, but no law states that it must be you.

- ◆ Start the meeting by focusing on relationships – create a ritual in which it's natural for you to spend just a little time reviewing the previous meeting.

- ◆ Allow each topic owner to indicate the desired outcome of their subject, how long they think they need, and what success looks like from their perspective.

CHAPTER SIX

The Zen of Facilitation

Merriam-Webster defines *facilitate* as "to make something easier" or "to help something run more smoothly or effectively." And while the second definition is more to the point, we like the first one too. When you run even a one-hour meeting, you are facilitating – the same thing you are trying to accomplish in your two-day meeting. You're trying to move the meeting along, make it run more smoothly, limit sidebar conversations, etc.

But this isn't an easy task, nor is it a skill we're born with. And your success with a two-day meeting will be greatly determined not only by the planning you've done but also by the way that you run the meeting. A well-planned, poorly-run meeting not only won't help, it may well hurt and cause you to be discredited before you even start. We offer some tips on how to facilitate a meeting. These are by no means exhaustive, so we'll recommend some books and certifications that will help you.

Distinguishing Being a Facilitator from Using a Facilitative Style

Facilitators serve as guides, leaders, and enablers:

- ◆ They play an important part in a well-run meeting by ensuring that the meeting is productive, focused, inclusive, and effective.

- They have skills in planning agendas, creating productive group environments, developing appropriate group processes, encouraging participation, and leading the group to reach its desired outcomes.

Instructors or leaders using a facilitative style are guides, instigators, partners, and leaders:

- They are experts in both content and process.

- They are tasked to ensure that the learners' direction and decisions are on target.

- They are responsible for motivating learners and creating a positive learning environment.

Facilitation Tips

- **Begin with the end in mind.** So sayeth Stephen Covey in his book *The Seven Habits of Highly Effective People.* If you keep your goals in mind during the meeting and remind the group of what they are on a regular basis, you'll increase your chances of success. *Do not allow yourself to be sidetracked.*

- **Be – or delegate someone to be – a timekeeper.** You have an agenda, and to the extent that it's humanly possible, you must get through it. Be firm about the time without being needlessly harsh. If something requires fifteen extra minutes, make a judgment call as to whether or not to allow it. Then make adjustments to the agenda accordingly.

- **Set expectations.** This should have been done pre-meeting. Do what salespeople do – tell them what you're going to tell them, tell them, then tell them what you told them.

- **In line with setting expectations, set ground rules.** This could include how long people get the floor (see "Meeting Goblins," below) and guidelines for breaks, device use, and starting right on time even if all are not present.

- **Be large and in charge.** Facilitating a two-day meeting with a number of people, some of whom may be senior to you, isn't for the faint of heart. Act like you belong there. This is your party.

A show of confidence is important and, oddly, can build more confidence.

- **Don't worry about being liked.** This isn't Facebook and you're not looking for likes. If you say to yourself, *If I stop this conversation they won't like me,* you're the wrong person not only for this meeting but also for a project manager job.

- **Be a good listener.** People need to be heard. Listen to them and don't just wait for your opening to speak. Try active listening, where you paraphrase back what they've said.

- **Manage conflict.** This is one of the tougher ones. Sometimes conflicts are of a long-standing nature, have nothing to do with the meeting, and aren't going to be *resolved* in this meeting. You and the sponsor should have discussed this in advance. Conflict doesn't necessarily (or even) mean that tempers flare. Conflict is to be expected, and as long as it's about issues and not personal, it can be very good for innovation and problem-solving.

- **If tempers flare, call for a break** – even if you've just had one.

- **Keep the conversation interesting.** Some people will come to the meeting expecting to be bored to tears for two days. Prevent this from happening. Engage them. Get stimulating conversation going about the product or the project. Use (very short) stories as appropriate.

- **Be flexible.** Remember how we said that you should have an agenda and that you must stick to it? Well, sure. But don't be afraid to tear it up or revise it mid-stream if you think adjustments need to be made.

- **Seek neutrality.** As likely as not, you're an internal employee working in a specific department. So, strictly speaking, neutrality is impossible. Unless you hire an outside facilitator, try to wear the other group's hat.

- **Allow the difficult discussions.** But if they blossom into subjects unto themselves, set another meeting to resolve that difficulty.

- **Demonstrate sensitivity and tactfulness.** Much of this comes from being a good listener, approachable, and laser-focused on meeting (and project) objectives.

- ◆ **Use humor wisely.** *Humor* doesn't mean having a Dilbert cartoon every third slide. *Humor* means saying something funny, witty, insightful, unexpected, and very particular to your location or team – even if you're outrageous once in a while. It helps a lot, especially in tense moments.

- ◆ **Admit that you don't know everything.** We're both instructors. Students expect us to know everything. But we don't. And so while it's tempting to bluff your way through an answer, refrain mightily from doing that. An occasional "I'm not sure, let me get back to you on that" isn't a failure on your part. Rather, it demonstrates that you know what you don't know.

- ◆ **Watch your (and others') non-verbal communication.** It's never good when someone folds their arms across their chest or turns a cold shoulder toward you. Learn to read the signs. If you'd like to use a little humor, tell your attendees that you're an expert at reading body language, and that you, for example, recognize that a "forehead on table" indicates that the meeting may have gone on a bit too long.

All of this guidance is well and good. But is it good enough? What makes meetings, well, *meetings*, is that they're collections of people. And some people, at least sometimes, are monsters.

The Meeting Goblins

As you've seen from the anecdotes in this book, there are all sorts of challenges to facilitating a project meeting. Some come from your physical environment, such as uncontrolled (or just uncomfortable) temperature in the room, faulty imaging or internet systems, or local (or very distant) noise such as drilling from a construction project on the floor above you, or a toilet flushing (seemingly forever) from halfway around the world. But most facilitation challenges originate from the monster-like behavior of human beings – we call them Meeting Goblins. You know them. They interrupt your meeting or derail it. They show up late or start side conversations. They grunt or grumble, they contradict you or others at the meeting, and, in the worst case, they even bully you or other participants.

Facilitators need to squelch our built-in propensity to be really nice people and to effectively handle these kinds of behaviors – directly and quickly, even at the risk of insulting or chasing away a Goblin. In effect, we're being not nice to the other participants by letting the Goblins hijack the meeting. Here are some ways in which you can deal with Meeting Goblins, and how you can even bring aboard other attendees as allies in the Great Meeting Goblin Wars!

The Flow Goblin

Let's start with the macro disrupters – Goblins who arrive too late or too early, make frequent exits and entrances, or are constantly missing meetings. They're disrupting the flow of the meeting, which is why we call them Flow Goblins. In the scenarios below, we'll call this Goblin (what else) Flo. When meeting attendance is an issue, here are some things you might do:

- Set ground rules about attendance; get a commitment from people that they will attend. Perhaps start your meeting officially at five minutes past the hour, noting that other meetings scheduled to end at the top of the hour often go over. Some companies even customize Outlook and other meeting scheduling software to make these sorts of adjustments automatically.

- If Flo is an habitual latecomer or, if it's a problem, an early-arriver, speak to her one-on-one after the meeting. Don't stop the meeting or go back to review something if Flo arrives late. She's late. If you review what she missed, she's making fifteen other people late. Ask one of the attendees to catch Flo up after the meeting. Or better yet, do it yourself.

- At the end of the meeting, take a moment to review the upcoming schedule and reconfirm availability.

- Don't be shy about going to Flo's functional (line) manager once you've exhausted the other possibilities. Just state the facts and the effects of Flo's *behavior* on the meetings and the project objectives; don't make it a personal attack.

The Garrulous Goblin

Now let's deal with the Garrulous Goblin – we'll call him Gary – who talks too long, or just too much, or in any way that seems to reduce participation by the fuller set of attendees. Here are some tips for addressing issues caused by Gary:

- It's okay to interject, and perhaps rather boisterously, "Thank you, Gary, we hear you. We need to get a wide variety of opinions on this issue." Then, in the same breath, and pointing to one of the quieter participants, say, "Juanita, what do *you* think about this option?"

- Remind Gary, and everyone else, of the agenda and the need to make the most use of your limited time together.

- It's very possible that Gary only wants attention, so don't spend a lot of time giving Gary eye contact. Or use the opposite approach – overdo it. Go right over to Gary and hover. Gary may back off.

- Write down what Gary said (the main point) on the whiteboard. Gary may then feel that he's literally left his mark and give up the floor.

- Institute a time limit for each person, perhaps two minutes per person. Hopefully this is in your ground rules already, but if it's not, nothing prevents you from improvising.

- Before the discussion starts, pose a standard for the length of comments. For example: "Let's hear from a few people for no more than two minutes each."

- Call for a break. Say, "You know what? I'll make sure I capture what Gary says, but (looking at watch), I think it's time for a biological break. See you back here in ten minutes." While you capture what Gary says, address the issue with him (privately and directly) about with the effect he's having on the meeting.

NOTE: We made Gary a male for a very specific reason. Pay attention, men: According to a George Washington University study (Hancock and Rubin 2014), when men were talking with women, they interrupted them 33 percent more often than when talking with men. The men interrupted women 2.1 times in a three-minute conversation, dropping to 1.8 times in a male-to-male conversation. Women interrupted men as little as once in a three-minute conversation. This corroborates an older study from Stanford University (Zimmerman and West 1996).

The Tangent Goblin

A close cousin of the Garrulous Goblin is the Tangent Goblin. This Goblin is either focused on a personal agenda and continues to steer the conversation to her specific point (which is not on-topic) or simply has the habit of going off on tangents that aren't productive for your meeting's objectives. Let's call our Tangent Goblin Tina. How should you address issues caused by Tina:

- Say, "Tina, this is very interesting. Can you tell us how this relates to the risk response options we're discussing?"
- Use the time-limit ideas from the Garrulous Goblin, above.
- If all else fails, simply be direct. "Tina, we need to get back on schedule. We were discussing risk response options – any other ideas?" (Turning your head) "Cathy, didn't you have some ideas on this?"

The Bully Goblin

Some attendees are bullies. They may be bullying another attendee or you as a facilitator, or the objectives of the meeting (see the Naysayer Goblin below). If you're unlucky enough to have a Bully Goblin (we'll call him Billy), here's what you can consider doing and saying as a facilitator:

- Step 1: Stop the meeting and have a one-on-one conversation with Billy. Ask what's behind his severe criticism and be sure you express to him that it's coming across as an attack. If it's based on something from outside the meeting (which is likely) request that he leaves this baggage out of your project meeting. Ask Billy what the meeting – or the project – could do to address his underlying concern.

- Step 2 (only if Step 1 doesn't work): Call him out. Say, "Billy, I consider what you're doing to be bullying and we cannot tolerate that. Please focus on the issues and stop this behavior. You'll be more likely to make your point in a civil manner."

The Naysayer Goblin

You may have a Goblin who is constantly negative. Nothing you do is right, nothing works around here, the project has no chance of success, everything is falling apart. We'll call this person the Naysayer Goblin. They may simply always be pessimistic or they may have the extra attribute of being unnecessarily contradictory. What do you do with Naysayer Nancy?

- Let's start with the good things that Naysayer Nancy may bring to the meeting. You need a contrary view. You need someone to identify possible flaws in your thinking. So be careful with the other tips here because sometimes – and there's a bit of an art in determining when that time is – Naysayer Nancy is helping you!

- Use a little humor. In one meeting in which one of us had a Naysayer Goblin, he simply said, "You know, Nancy – the pessimists are always *eventually* right. Rome fell, and the dinosaurs went extinct, but they both had a good run. Let's focus on the specific ways in which we can improve this project." That actually muted Naysayer Nancy.

- Challenge Nancy to give three examples of good or successful things about the project.

- Don't let Nancy give out a laundry list of all that's wrong with the project. After she's dropped a couple of negatives on the meeting, say "Okay, Nancy, can you stop right there and give us some suggestions on how we can fix those first two problems?"

The Chatty Goblin

Some folks can't help having side conversations with their neighbor, and this can be annoying and disruptive. We'll call this the Chatty Goblin, and we'll call him Charlie. It's no coincidence that you may recognize some of the corrections for Chatty Charlie from your middle-school English teacher . . .

- Say "Charlie – I see you have something to say, would you mind sharing it with the entire group?"

- Just stop talking, halt the meeting, and direct everyone to stare at the people having the side conversation.

- Tap the table (or maybe pound it!) and say, "We need to have one meeting here!"

- Walk over to Charlie and his conversation partner (who is probably going to be relieved that you're freeing her from Charlie's speech). Your close presence will probably be enough.

- Reiterate the ground rules, which, hopefully, discourage side conversations.

- Remember – people will respect you for keeping the meeting on track. In fact, they'll be looking (literally) at you to do that. If you don't, they'll lose respect for you.

The bottom line is that sometimes people come to a meeting with an agenda and it's not *your* agenda. Often people feel that, in life or in their job, they're not being heard. Maybe they've witnessed project after project fail and they want to make sure that you understand this. Let them be heard, but let them know that their ideas must be expressed in a constructive manner.

That's a quick summary of ways to improve the facilitation of your meeting. We're sure it can help you now. And Zen.

We'll leave this chapter with one final tip: Sometimes in meetings you're a problem-solver, and that means that you need to understand the causes of the problems and not just the symptoms. Admittedly, your attendees aren't six-year-old problem children on an airplane, but the poem below, which features a six-year-old problem child, goes a long way in explaining *how you may have to think* to reconcile troublesome meeting attendees.

A gentleman traveling on a coast-to-coast flight
Was the kind of a person who had real insight.
A six-year-old youngster was really a fright
Running up and down aisles and giving a fight.

The people in business were trying to work
Near those who were sleeping, the youngster did lurk.
He yanked off the headsets of some music lovers,
And took all of the peanuts that he could discover.

The passengers complained, "He must be controlled."
And threatened the flight crew to knock him out cold.
The flight attendant buckled him into his seat
But his screams and his hollers were less than a treat.

The passengers, desperate, want him bound tight and gagged;
"Arrest the boy's parents, or let them be nagged."
At last comes our gentleman, who spoke to the crew.
They loved his idea; into action they flew.

They found a seat for the boy in the front of the plane.
They were willing to do it to keep themselves sane.
They fashioned a steering wheel from a large plate;
A stick was a rudder; he thought it was great.

Flying instruments were made from some odds and some ends.
The pilot came back; the two became friends.
The pilot then asked for help flying the plane
Because it'd be tough if they ran into rain.

The kid was delighted; he was taught how to fly.
Flight attendants all smiled; the copilot came by.
The pilot saluted and left the boy in command.
He kept pretty quiet and thought it was grand.

The passengers rejoiced; the gentleman was praised.
"How did you think of it?" the question was raised.
The gentleman answered in a voice calm and low,
"It's really quite simple, if you go with the flow.

You tried hard to solve your own problem, the noise;
But the problem I solved was that of the boy's."

— *Janice Y. Preston, CPA, PMP*

CHAPTER SEVEN

Case Study: Building a House

W E REALIZE THAT THE ARTIFACTS created in this book may seem a little abstract, so we created this case study that we'll refer to throughout the rest of the book so that you can see how our ideas are applied in the real world. One of us has co-written a book called *Green Project Management*, so we thought it would be interesting if we gave you an example that relates to a project focused on sustainability.

Our story features fictitious Mayor Karyn Salas of Escondido, California, a city of about 150,000 people about thirty miles north of San Diego, with a median age of thirty three years. With the passage of the Global Warming Solutions Act of 2006, California has become a world leader in progressive legislation aimed at curbing climate change. The bill requires California to roll back its greenhouse gas emissions to 1990 levels by the year 2020, and it provides a framework for achieving that goal in a quantifiable and cost-effective way while boosting economic growth through green job creation.

In our story, Mayor Salas is nearing the end of her first term and is seeking re-election in an area where ecological concerns are front and center in the young electorate. Her platform calls for further buy-in to the Go Green Escondido program, started by her staff near the end of her first year in office. Ms. Salas has been an advocate of sustainable building, and she wants to demonstrate her commitment by building her own new home using the techniques she's been promoting.

She referred to "Green Principles for Residential Design" (Sustainable Buildings Industry Council 2016) for ideas and decided to implement several of these green building ideas into her own home – very publicly. After all, what's a project but a conversion of ideas into reality? In particular, she's decided to focus on making these three ideas into reality:

- **Minimizing energy use and using renewable energy strategies.** This principle covers aspects such as the importance of dramatically reducing the overall energy loads (through insulation, efficient equipment and lighting, and careful detailing of the entire enclosure), limiting the amount of fossil fuels required, incorporating renewable energy systems such as photovoltaics, geothermal heat pumps, and solar water heating whenever feasible, and purchasing green power in order to minimize the creation of greenhouse gasses.

- **Conserving and protecting water.** This principle covers aspects such as reducing, controlling, or treating site runoff; designing and constructing the home to conserve water used inside and outside; and minimizing leaks by ensuring proper inspections during construction.

- **Using environmentally preferable products.** This principle covers such aspects as specifying products that are salvaged, are made with recycled content, are easily disassembled for reuse or recycling, conserve natural resources, reduce overall material use, are exceptionally durable or low maintenance, are naturally or minimally processed, save energy and/or water, and/or reduce pollution or waste from operations.

From these principles, she has chosen to integrate three related elements into her home construction project, with the thinking that they should be accessible technologies that others could readily implement, rather than over-reaching and building a wind farm or seeking Leadership in Energy and Environmental Design (LEED) platinum qualification for her house. Those elements include:

- Installing a Tesla solar roof
- Installing a rainwater capture system for non-potable use (such as irrigation)
- Installing a hot tub
- Selecting a maximum of recycled and salvaged materials as described above, adding a step to the purchasing process in which she and a team of college interns from nearby Cal State University, San Marcos, oversee the selection of materials

Now that you have the background of this case study you'll understand how it relates to productive planning meetings when you read the following chapters.

CHAPTER EIGHT

Preparing for the Project Planning Meeting

NOTE: Before you plan and schedule your meeting, be sure that there aren't any looming unaddressed issues that might crop up during the meeting. Engage the sponsor in this, since he or she will need to be involved and may likely already be aware of any problems. The last thing you want is to go to all the time and trouble to set up a project planning meeting and instead wind up overseeing a grievance meeting or a power struggle. Either deal with that first or plan on having a three-day meeting, the first day of which could be a clearing-the-air session. The meeting should take place with the expectation that you'll get the best out of the people who attend.

L ET'S BE HONEST – the project planning meeting is going to cost you time and money to host. So you want to be absolutely, positively, 100 percent ready to have a good meeting, and to get a strong return on your investment. People hate to go to one-hour meetings and have their time wasted. Imagine if they fly in from around the world, only to find that you don't have your act together. *This is the person*, they will ask themselves, perhaps even in italics, *who's going to run our project*?

So you must take time out of your busy schedule and plan for this thoroughly. Here are some questions to ask yourself:

- ◆ **Who's facilitating the meeting?** Is it you? Is it your project manager? If so, does he or she have the facilitation (not to mention people) skills necessary to undertake such an endeavor? If not, consider hiring someone who can do this. It doesn't have to be a professionally certified facilitator. It does, however, need to be someone who knows how to run a large meeting, understands the issues, and can keep the team on focus. You don't want a person who has a strong need to be liked running your meeting.

- ◆ **Who's attending the meeting?** This is key. For our house-building project, we'll want the plumber, the electrician, the architect, the HVAC people, etc. If it's a pharmaceutical project, you'll want the various functions in attendance, so include research, marketing, packaging, manufacturing, regulatory, etc. And, of course, be sure to invite the sponsor. Get the right people in the right room so that the right discussions can be had and the right decisions made. Be sure to engage the people who'll get their hands dirty, or, at the very least, be sure that someone attends who can properly represent their issues and concerns. The converse is also true: if you leave someone out you may hear them utter the dreaded phrase, "I wish you had asked *me*. I would have told you that you had to get an XYZ Permit before you could dig those trenches. Harrumph!"

- ◆ **Do you have an agenda?** Make sure you have an agenda and that you've published it in advance (see Exhibit 8.1). On the one hand, this agenda must be airtight so that everyone knows what's happening and when. On other hand, it should be flexible enough so that it can be torn up and rearranged if circumstances dictate. Prior to the meeting, call and/or email everyone and ask them if they've seen the agenda. Ask them if they have any questions or concerns. Do not leave this to chance. Do not leave *anything* to chance. You might hope that things will go well, but, to quote a cliché, hope is not a strategy.

Recalling our section "Be Sensory," and using our case study example, Karyn may well want to have a large artist's-conception drawing of her home up on the wall for everyone to see while the meeting goes on. Not only will it be a way to point out specific elements ("the roof is the

Sample Agenda

MEETING OBJECTIVES

- Gain full team understanding of the project
- Create the initial project schedule
- Create the initial list of risks along with risk response plans
- Validate the initial schedule and risk plan with the team
- Surface (and resolve) any resourcing issues

Outcomes of the Meeting

- A project with a significantly improved chance of success, due to a thoughtful and far-reaching plan
- Understanding of each team's perspective, roles, and responsibilities and a shared vision for the project's deliverables
- Buy-in from all key stakeholders

Deliverables of the Meeting

- A work breakdown structure (WBS) for each function
- Initial (draft) schedule
- Initial list of risks/issues
- RACI– detail level will depend on available time

PREWORK

- Provide detailed estimates as per attached guidelines
- Provide documented functional strategies (clinical, marketing, regulatory)
- Review project documentation sent to you:
    - Current integrated schedule
    - Product definition document
- Bring with you your current project documentation and strategy presentations

DRESS

- Business casual (working meeting)

Exhibit 8.1. A Sample Agends: Sending a comprehensive agenda to participants prior to the meeting is a key to success.

DAY ONE		
Start Time	**Item**	**Who**
8:00	Review agenda, discuss objective for the meeting, Introduce critical success factors	Sponsor
8:15	Introduce the project, present initial RACI, communications plan, risk register	Sponsor/Project manager
8:45	Presentations by the individual groups	TBD
9:45	BREAK	
10:00	Presentation of how to do a WBS	Project manager
10:30	Development of individual WBSs	All in groups
12:00	LUNCH	
12:30	WBS development continued	Small Groups
14:00	Check-in	All
14:15	BREAK	
14:30	Schedule development continues	All
17:00	Day One conclusions & check-in (large team)	All
17:30	END	
	Evening activity	

Exhibit 8.1 (cont.). Agenda items for day one include start times and who is expected to attend each session.

part here on the top"), it will serve as a reminder of the end product of the project. A not-so-subtle additional visual could be a "Salas 2020" campaign banner.

Meeting Agenda Tips

- **Emphasize that the meeting will start *on time*.** If in reality you give a five- or ten-minute grace period for traffic issues, etc., that's fine. Have a conference bridge set up. (We'll discuss virtual methods of attendance in chapter 10.) Latecomers who are stuck in traffic can dial in and attend virtually until they arrive (safely, perhaps as a passenger or pulled over, rather than as a distracted driver). Make sure that mobile dial-in participants are on mute

DAY TWO		
Start Time	Item	Who
9:00	Schedule development continues: linking interdependencies, identifying missed activities	All
10:00	BREAK	
10:15	Group discussion of draft schedule, action items	
10:45	Schedule development continues: breakout sessions as required to discuss technical or other issues	
12:00	LUNCH	
12:30	Review of schedule, open discussion	All
13:30	Risk management plan 　－　Identify and rank risks 　－　Develop initial risk management strategies Note: This element may be facilitated parallel to some people continuing with the schedule development, if needed.	
15:00	BREAK	
15:45	Schedule compression/adjustment/ tradeoffs (if required)	
16:45	Closing statement by sponsor and next steps	
17:00	ADJOURN	

Exhibit 8.1 (cont.). Agenda items for day two include start times, who is expected to attend each session, and when the meeting will adjourn.

unless they need to speak; this avoids interrupting the meeting with honking and expletives from drivers.

- **Have a risk response plan for this two-day project.** What if there's a power failure? Or an emergency? Or an unexpected weather condition? Have a Plan B in your pocket. Make sure you have a spare projector or projector replacement bulb or LED. Bring your own laptop, even if the facility has a PC. Think of *everything* that can go wrong and have a backup. Not only is this good practice for your risk planning, but it will demonstrate that

43

you "walk the talk" when it comes to project management. You don't want someone to say – to themselves or, even worse, out loud – "They can't even run a meeting. How are they going to run this large, multinational project?"

- **Plan for two full days, from 8 a.m. to 5:30 p.m.** If you publish an agenda that shows everyone adjourning at 3:30 on Day Two, everyone will set their watch by that. Conversely, if you say that you're going to adjourn at 5:30 on the second day and actually wrap up by 4:00, they'll love you and carry you out on their shoulders, singing your praises.

- **Ask attendees to give this matter their full attention.** Everyone will have other meetings they should be attending. As much as possible, ask them not to schedule any during this time. Some people will have meetings they absolutely cannot miss. This is fine, but address these issues on Day One so that you can anticipate absences and work around them.

- **Set expectations.** Your attendees are, for all intents and purposes, your *stakeholders*. You want there to be no doubt as to why you're convening. The last thing you need is people showing up and saying, "I thought we were going to discuss the color of the house." No, that's a requirement and should have already been determined. You're there for specific reasons, and they shouldn't be a secret.

    That said – and this is important – don't ignore your stakeholders if one of them says, "Yes, I know the house is green but I'd still like to go over it." Build some buffer time into your schedule for the unexpected.

- **Address hidden agendas.** Not everyone on your project team is necessarily as enthusiastic about your project as you are (see Exhibit 8.2). If you know that, say, Bob over in operations finds your project to be a threat to him, best to know that now and address it with the sponsor. The sponsor may know that already. The sponsor needs (or you both need) to have a conversation with Bob and perhaps with his boss. You don't need anybody to sabotage your project, and certainly not starting right here at this meeting.

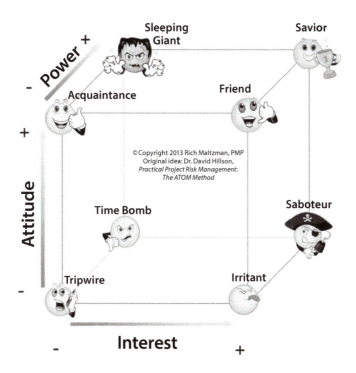

Exhibit 8.2. Meeting attendees may have hidden agendas – know what they are and deal with them if possible. Adapted from David Hillson and Peter Simon, *Practical Project Risk Management: The Atom Method.*

- **Hold a preliminary phone call (or two).** Let people ask questions. Listen intently to their concerns. They're much easier to correct at the pre-meeting stage than in the middle of the meeting, or worse, during the execution of the project! The more that people understand your goals and the more that you get their buy-in, the smoother the meeting will go. You don't want someone sitting there saying, "I still don't understand why we're here." It affects the whole team. Don't call this meeting unless you're prepared to *sell it* to some extent. (Here's where the sponsor can be quite helpful.)

- **Decide who will be the scribe for the meeting.** Every single word that's spoken doesn't have to be written down. But someone will need to summarize the meeting and notate outcomes, actions taken, actions assigned, etc. If it has to be the project manager, so be it, but it's best if you have someone else, someone who has no other specific role.

- **Assign pre-work as necessary.** Some and possibly all teams may want to do a presentation. Sometimes, if it's a technical solution you're working on, a team member may have to bring a proto-type. Make sure that everyone understands their pre-work, and follow up with them as needed to ensure that they're prepared. Have team members bring several printed copies of their (brief) presentations. That way they can still speak if there's a last-minute problem with the projector. Provide everyone with a standardized template so they can address the same things. People may not like having homework to do before the meeting, but they'll thank you later when they are saving three to four hours of pre-work every night for five weeks because this meeting has properly clarified the project's schedule, scope, risk, and/or resource requirements.

- **You yourself may have some pre-work to do.** On at least one of our engagements, the customer wanted to pre-create the work breakdown structures in order to save time in the session. We also suggest starting an initial list of risks. There are *always* risks (not enough resources, time, budget) so it's best to put those on the table right away. Seed some opportunities as well as threats to start a thread of discussion on the things that could go horri-bly right on your project. Your sponsor, and work-wizened contributors from similar projects, can be a great source of this in-formation. And, if you have it, historical information from other projects, such as lessons learned, can be of great assistance.

- **Pre-populate an initial list of assumptions.** Projects are limited by constraints (time, budget, resources) but also by assumptions (for example, we'll have the senior developer available, or 75 percent of Mary's time will be devoted to this project.) The best thing to do is get these assumptions out in the open. They'll be challenged, and they'll also (hopefully) be intelligently supple-mented. Take advantage of lessons learned from prior projects – your list of assumptions can come from a prior, similar project.

In our case study, Karyn should find other examples of sustainable home construction to help populate the assumption log. The latest edition of the *PMBOK® Guide*, by the way, formalizes this in two ways: it has a new process called Manage Project Knowledge, and there's a document called an Assumption Log, purpose-built to record assumptions.

- **Stay as focused on possible on the most important artifacts.** Since your goal is to produce certain artifacts in a very limited amount of time, stay laser-focused on that list. Nevertheless, it's often advantageous to request that different functions prepare a ten-minute talk on the project (challenges, issues) from their perspective. It gives them a voice and also engages them and other team members. Very often you'll find that there are chronic problems – for example, team members may already be oversubscribed on other projects. The sponsor and the whole team need to hear this.

- **Make sure you have all the project prerequisites.** In order to do the work of this planning session, you must have certain information. For example, requirements for the product or service should be fairly well-understood. One of us worked on a project wherein the requirements had not been established and it then made it challenging to produce a schedule. In that case we had to bring in another consultant to run a requirements-gathering session which prevented us from achieving the full meeting objectives. In our house-building case, we need to know that the house is a ranch that will have, say, three bedrooms, an indoor pool, and a two-car garage. If some at the meeting believe it's that, and others believe it's a split-level with two bedrooms, no pool, and no garage, you'll spend all your time figuring that out instead of doing the proposed work of the meeting.

- **Get RACI.** *RACI* stands for responsible, accountable, consulted, and informed. It's a type of responsibility assignment matrix. Create a preliminary version for your project, using our template, which is based on your best assumptions going into the meeting. When you display it, it's entirely possible that some team member will say, "Which project that I'm currently working on should I give up to do this one?" Your sponsor may not want to hear that, but that's exactly what she needs to hear. This gives the sponsor a chance to either negotiate with the functional manager or find another resource. See our Glossary and Refresher appendices for a definition, and some more guidance, on RACI.

- **Decide on ground rules.** In a multi-day session, it's almost impossible for people to refrain from using their electronic devices – all of them are working on something else. Try giving them a break every seventy-five minutes or so to let them check their mail. Invariably there will be someone who's in the middle of a crucial project, so you may have to make an exception to the rules. There should also be ground rules about etiquette – you want a productive session, not a "let's bash the marketing group while we're here" diatribe. There will be disagreement and arguments, which can be good energy, as long as it's focused. We like to refer to Graham's Hierarchy of Disagreement to understand the different ways that people disagree (see Exhibit 8.3). Show this graphic to your team, and make sure you're always aiming at the peak and staying away from the base.

- **Make sure all your technology works in advance.** Ensure that your Wi-Fi works and that everyone has the password; put it on a flip chart, otherwise people will forget and ask you every five minutes to remind them what it is.

  Also, test your virtual connectivity (see chapter 10 for virtual attendance tips). Test anything that should be functioning on the day of the meeting (different browsers can produce wildly unpredictable results). Otherwise, instead of getting work done, half the room is involved in getting your wireless mouse to work. That's great teamwork, but not the best use of the experts you've assembled. Also, mitigate a possibly embarrassing scenario by turning off notifications from Twitter, Facebook, Outlook, and/ or Skype (for example). Nobody (least of all you) wants to see the meeting interrupted by a pop-up notice indicating that someone's anti-flatulence meds have arrived, or that their very specific dating service has found a match.

48

Graham's Hierarchy of Disagreement

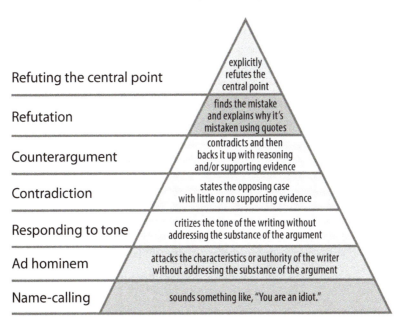

Refuting the central point	explicitly refutes the central point
Refutation	finds the mistake and explains why it's mistaken using quotes
Counterargument	contradicts and then backs it up with reasoning and/or supporting evidence
Contradiction	states the opposing case with little or no supporting evidence
Responding to tone	critizes the tone of the writing without addressing the substance of the argument
Ad hominem	attacks the characteristics or authority of the writer without addressing the substance of the argument
Name-calling	sounds something like, "You are an idiot."

Exhibit 8.3. In this hierarchy of disagreement, Paul Graham presents a seven-level prioritized list of how people disagree well (or not so well).

♦ **Decide where to hold the meeting.** In a perfect world, we suggest holding it off-site at a nearby hotel conference room. This gets everyone away from their work environment and allows them to focus. If your budget won't allow for this, try to act as a barrier to outside interruptions on behalf of the group. This means that you may have to personally contact attendees' functional managers and make sure they understand what's going on during this meeting and why it's so important.

Wherever you decide to hold the meeting, be sure you know what's going on in the facility during that period of time, and plan around it. Also take into consideration religious and school holidays when doing your planning. One of us has taught project management classes at hotels and business centers frequently.

49

Thus far he has encountered everything from leaf-blowers out-side the room, to trucks that beep when they back up, to fire drills happening during practice tests.

- **Plan to have lunch catered every day.** Make sure you have plenty of coffee, tea, and snacks. Don't load up on donuts that no one will eat; try fresh fruit and yogurt instead. Mitigate risk by checking beforehand with attendees about dietary restrictions, allergies, and preferences. A little homework goes a long way, even though you can't please everyone.

- **Make sure you have the right materials.** You'll need the following:

  - Flip charts – one for each group, one for the facilitator, and one (at least) for parking lot items

  - Markers for all functions in various colors – brand new and not dried-out and left over from 1950, like the ones most hotel conference rooms seem to provide

  - Sticky notes of various sizes and colors

  - Adhesive tape

  - Name tags or tent cards if team members have never met

  - Wireless access and power strips

  - Notepads and pens

  - Spare laptop

  You're going to be doing a lot of hands-on work, putting flip charts on the wall and taping the sticky notes down. Make sure there's enough usable wall surface. It sounds silly, but you also may want to make sure that flipcharts will stick to the walls. A visit to the hotel in advance to sort all of this out will greatly help. Hotels can be hit-or-miss in their support of conferences, saving their best customer service for their overnight guests. You're paying for the room, so you deserve good service. Make sure you talk to the manager.

- **Have the support you'll need.** Make sure your administrative assistant is on top of things and can run out and get anything you need. If you're holding the meeting internally, have phone numbers for IT support.

- **Set a dress code.** It should mirror your company's culture, but make sure people are dressed comfortably but not sloppily. And suggest that people bring a light sweater, no matter what the time of year. Temperatures in rooms (especially in hotels) can fluctuate wildly. Trust us; you do not want to spend half of your time turning the thermostat up or down. Layers of clothing are a form of risk response to the threat of The Great Battle For Temperature Control.

- **Check the room setup.** You might want to set the room up initially as a large roundtable, or long tables in a U-shape, and later break it down into pods, or teams, working together. Think this through in advance. Again, you don't want to spend time deciding on these things during the meeting. The bottom line: do not be *surprised* by your room! Hotels host meetings routinely, and they can provide you with just about any room configuration you would like.

- **Set up a document repository in advance.** If you're using a repository tool such as SharePoint, make sure it's set up pre-meeting. Upload all the artifacts you'll be using in the meeting, and make sure the team knows it's there and how to use it. Everyone should be able to access it inside and outside of firewalls.

- **Publish a roster.** It should include names, roles, and contract information for each team member. Make sure it's in your repository. This will become an important project artifact.

- **Create a communications plan using our template (see Appendix F).** Display this or pass it around during the meeting. After people leave the meeting, they'll need to know how and when communications will occur. If you're the project manager, the team needs to understand your approach to managing the project.

- **Expect resistance.** The team needs to understand what a facilitator's role is (one of us worked on a project where the group even questioned the *need* for a facilitator). *The meeting does not run itself.* Don't assume that everyone knows what you know. Also, don't assume that they're as excited about your project as you are. They have a million other things to do, so take that into consideration.

One of the authors scheduled a meeting to plan a project that would involve a facility in the southeast United States. Everything was planned to a T, and all the right people were invited, including the vendors. This was only a half-day meeting, but we still had the objective of creating a draft schedule. Everyone was on board except . . . the woman who "owned" the facility. She was a manager of that site, and her basic comment was, "We've done a million of these pilots, each one worse than the last. Why should I do this one? What are your goals?" And you know what? She was absolutely right. She was a major stakeholder, and no one had ever reached out to her; they just assumed that she would be on board.

The good news was that, even though we didn't meet our meeting objectives, the meeting turned into a good opportunity to talk about some important issues, and we adjourned after two hours instead of four. (We could have lived without airing dirty laundry in front of the vendors, though.)

- **Plan a fun activity for the evenings.** It could be attending, or even participating in, a sporting event or a dinner. Socializing gives team members a chance to get to know each other better outside of the work environment. This is when the pictures of the kids, dogs, iguanas, and cats come out, which is all to the group's benefit – consider it an important part of the team Forming stage of team building. Escape rooms, where teams have an hour to find clues to escape a room, have turned out to be quite popular lately. The downside, of course, is that if the team doesn't find the clues, they're stuck in that room for the rest of their lives. Don't go to a movie – make sure the event is something where team members interact.

- **Pay attention to logistics, directions, and security.** We've lost track of the number of times we've been invited to a meeting and been given simple directions, only to discover that "137 Main Street" represented a complex of twelve business condominiums. And once we found the building, we discovered that no one at the front desk knew who we were, *and* we had to go through security, get a badge, etc.

You want to avoid this situation at all costs. The last thing you need at a meeting is people showing up an hour late, angry because they had no idea how to find the building, never mind the conference room. Make sure they all have your mobile number and be sure to check it frequently. Remember that some people are last-minute Louies, and will leave for the meeting roughly around the time it's supposed to start.

Logistics are important. Personally make sure that attendees know the address, the building number, and any security restrictions (for example, the need for badges), assuming that your meeting is in-house. Suggest that attendees get there early so they can navigate this situation. Be sure the front desk (or security, if in-house) has a list of all attendees. (If you don't know how to do this, find somebody in the company who has done it before.

Also be sure that all attendees have several cell phone numbers – yours, your assistant's, and, for good measure, the most reliable person you can think of, as a backup. Whether or not getting in the door goes perfectly, your backup measures will impress everybody.

◆ **Use a planning meeting readiness checklist.** It will help ensure that you don't miss a step. The sponsor should review the checklist and sign off on it. (See Exhibit 8.4 on the next page.)

Planning Meeting Readiness Checklist

- ☐ Facilitator and, if need be, co-facilitator chosen
- ☐ Attendee list decided on and reviewed by sponsor
- ☐ Agenda created and published
- ☐ Preliminary phone call(s) done
- ☐ Facilitator pre-work completed
- ☐ Project or product requirements understood
- ☐ Project charter and scope statement created
- ☐ Pre-work assigned
- ☐ Initial list of risks created
- ☐ Initial Assumption Log created
- ☐ Relevant information from previous projects
- ☐ Front desk and security logistics complete and communicated
- ☐ Room Logistics verified
- ☐ Preliminary work assigned
- ☐ SharePoint or other common area available for document sharing

Exhibit 8.4. Use this checklist to make sure you're ready for your planning meeting (and the meeting sponsor should sign off on it). Expand the list as needed.

CHAPTER NINE

Facilitating the Project Planning Meeting

I f you've followed all the precepts in the previous chapter, you should be well set up to move forward. Let's look at the meeting itself in detail.

Day One

Pre-session

Arrive early and make sure the room is set up to your specifications. You should have ordered breakfast for everyone (a light selection of pastries and coffee is fine). As people filter in, greet them and make them feel welcome. This may seem unnecessary, but these stakeholders are your guests – treat them as such. And that guy who may be most opposed to your project? Treat him the best.

Don't panic if, say, the projector doesn't work. There's a lot of technology, a lot of it is new and ever-changing, and everyone is accustomed to technical glitches. What we've noticed is that people will be more put off by your panicked reaction than by the technical problem itself. However, it's best to be sure that you have the contact numbers for the audio/visual department handy so that you can get someone from there to fix it or replace it while you're making sure everything else is set up. Think of your administrative assistant, the hotel manager, the A/V people, and tech support as your team, who are there to help you resolve issues.

Session

Begin the session by welcoming everyone and thanking them for their time. Take a few minutes to reiterate why you're there and what you're hoping to accomplish. If you have a visual of the product of your project, such as the artist's conceptual drawing of Karyn's home, now is the time to draw the attendees' attention to it. No need to dwell on previous project failures that may have driven you to have this meeting in the first place. (Everyone already knows about them.) Have an upbeat, *can-do* attitude, and explain that this gathering will not only assist in getting the project off to a good start but will also help foster a team atmosphere. *Remember, your attitude is contagious.* (And see chapter 15 for advice on team building.)

Hand out and/or display the agenda on-screen. But don't just display it – make it clear that you are seeking full agreement on that agenda as your roadmap for the time you spend together. *Make sure that everyone is in agreement with it.* Let them know that there's some flexibility if adjustments have to be made. Sometimes a new element is introduced. For example, despite best intentions, it's possible that the sponsor may have heard from his boss the night before the meeting that now you need three bedrooms instead of two. Or maybe the budget is less than you anticipated. Don't let this derail you; instead, accept it as the normal flow of projects. Life isn't perfect. Remind the team that the perfect is the enemy of the good. Or the good enough.

Remind attendees that not all of them will be required all of the time for everything. If there are break-out sessions and their attendance isn't required, suggest that this is a good time for them to get some work done. Otherwise some people will, frankly, just sit around moping or checking email waiting for you to give them instruction. This is why a hotel is often an ideal off-site venue. Attendees can sit in the lobby and make calls, use wireless, etc. until their presence is required again.

Sponsor

After everyone is in place and set up, the sponsor should speak to the group. As discussed in the planning session, she now has a group in front of her and can deliver a non-project message or pep talk if so desired. Again, the caveat is that time taken away from the specifics of the project is at the expense of the creation of artifacts.

The sponsor's goal is to accomplish several things:

- **State, or re-state, the purpose of this session.** People want to know (and deserve to know) why you need two days of their time. You may have already said this prior to the meeting. But let's remind you of this adage (often attributed to Aristotle):
  - Tell them what you're going to tell them.
  - Tell them.
  - Tell them what you told them.

- **Empower the project manager.** Project managers in organizations often have no direct reports and, hence, little formal authority. So it must be clear from the beginning that the sponsor expects everyone in the room to follow the project manager's direction. This step is very important. It has probably already been said, but it won't hurt to have it reiterated.

- **Provide an overview of the project.** Sponsors are invariably at a senior level, so they typically have a better picture of how the project fits into the organization. What priority does it have? How does executive management see it? People like to be on projects that are not only interesting to work on but that have some import to the company.

  If it helps you, think of your project as one rolled-up task on a longer-term timeline that represents the overall portfolio of your organization.

- **Introduce the facilitator.** If the sponsor and/or project manager are facilitating, this step will be unnecessary. If you've hired a facilitator, the team needs to know exactly what his or her role is. And they need to know that they have your, and the facilitator's, full faith, confidence, and respect. Effectively, the facilitator's job is to move the meeting along and keep it on track.

- **Establish and enforce ground rules.** It's easy for some people to dominate a conversation and perhaps intimidate others. This must not happen, and it's the job of the facilitator to prevent it, with the enforcement of the sponsor if possible.

- **Answer questions.** No matter how well you prepare, people will have questions. The sponsor should endeavor to answer them as honestly as possible. Often the question will involve resources.

How, they will ask, can they accomplish this project as well as all the other ones they're working on? There's no set answer, but the question must be addressed. People are also very interested in your roadmap. What happens down the road?

◆ **Explain the process.** Many team members have never attended a session such as this. The sponsor should explain that the meeting and the artifacts it creates are part of a time-honored project management technique, and that it was decided to incorporate them as a gesture towards best practices. Given the sometimes haphazard way that projects are run in organizations, most will see this as a welcome change.

◆ **Review the critical success factors.** What elements need to be in place for the team to succeed? These elements might include quick access to the sponsor to resolve issues, a good communications plan, etc. Critical success factors are different from success criteria, or objectives, which are things such as "delivered on-time," "delivered on-budget," and "captured X percent of market." See our table in the Glossary appendix.

Project Manager and Sponsor (Project Management Lead)

Now that the groundwork has been set by the sponsor, it's incumbent upon the project manager to explain how the *project* will be run and what tools will be used. Take the time to explain this; in many organizations, best practices are not used to their full extent. Explain that you're doing this in order to have better control of the project in order to meet its objectives.

◆ **Schedule.** Whether you use Microsoft Project, Primavera, Excel, or some enterprise-wide project management software, it's greatly advantageous to show them what the schedule will look like when complete (begin with the end in mind). This is *not* training for the tool, just a way for them to see how the pieces all interact. So *show* them either a schedule from a previous project or a template. Reassure them that they don't have to learn this tool, but that they will have to provide input to it in order for you to maintain it and keep it up to date. You could even seed the room with a person who, on your signal, could talk positively about how well the scheduling system aided the last project they were on.

- **Communications plan.** Using our template, show the team how communications will flow. For example, there might be a weekly team meeting to discuss action items, schedule, and risks. There might be a monthly steering committee meeting to advise senior management of progress. There might be a lessons learned meeting at the end of each phase to determine what can be done better.

- **RACI matrix.** As we said earlier, this is one form of a responsibility assignment matrix, and it maps the what (the tasks of the project) to the who (the contributors to the project). *RACI* stands for responsible, accountable, consulted, and informed (see Exhibit 9.1), and at the intersection of the what and the who, defines just what the contributor contributes:
  - R: A direct task assignment – the person responsible
  - A: The "heads will roll" level of accountability
  - C: A person who must be consulted (perhaps for technical approval or legal counsel)
  - I: A person who should be informed (perhaps for courtesy or safety reasons

- **Risk register.** The sponsor (and possibly functional managers) should have been able to identify a list of preliminary risks. Display this and discuss how risk management will be an important part of your process going forward. Also explain that the team will be learning how to do risk analysis during this meeting, and that they will be developing a list of risks along with possible responses to those risks.

- **Change control form.** This one's a bit tricky. You should ideally have change control in your organization, and it should be applied to projects. Change control helps prevent scope creep. So ideally you'll have set up a change control mechanism with changes to be approved by a change control board or steering committee. People will really grumble at this one since everybody wants what they want when they want it. But by enforcing change control, you're protecting the integrity of the project. Share examples of projects that had the best of intentions but went way over budget, fell behind schedule, or both, or got

59

RACI MATRIX – HOUSE BUILDING PROJECT						
House Building Project	Architect	Plumber	Electrician	Environmental SME	Publicist	Project Manager
Identify a minimum of three contractors from Angie's List	A/R	–	–	–	–	I
Arrange contractor visits and quotations	A	–	–	–	–	R
Ensure all wiring is complete	C	I	A	–	–	I
Ensure that all components comply with LEED specs	I	I	–	A/R	I	I
Coordinate communications among all stakeholders	–	–	–	–	–	A/R
Ensure that all plumbing is complete	I	A	I	I	–	I
Investigate best solution for implementing cistern	C	C	I	A	–	C
Coordinate communications with press and campaign	C	–	–	C	A	C

Exhibit 9.1. This RACI matrix for our case study (a partial listing) maps the tasks of the project to the contributors to the project. Adapted from RACIchart.org.

canceled, because they failed to tame the insidious monster of scope creep. By the same token encourage attendees to understand that the project that *consciously* accepts new scope can be the one that brings more value to their stakeholders.

Functional Presentations

As mentioned in previous chapter, each contributing function (in our case study, that would be architects, electricians, plumbers, roofers) should be encouraged to provide a presentation on the project from their viewpoint. This presentation should be brief, but it needs to be to-the-point and effective. In our sample agenda, we set aside an hour for this (see Exhibit 8.1). It could be more or less time, depending on how many functions there are and how involved the technical details are. But it's up to the facilitator to make sure that things move along. This is an area where breakout sessions could be held by participants during the course of the two days if additional discussion is required. And, of course, impromptu sessions will occur. Let them.

Each presentation should drill down into several areas:

- **Team presentation.** Gives a chance to introduce the functional team to the larger group.

- **Technical aspects.** One of us did a lot of work in pharmaceutical organizations. Invariably one (or more) of the groups would talk about some drug or medical device issue. What if it's an IT project? Or R&D? If you're using cutting-edge technology, there may be some discussion needed to explain it to the group. And, by the way, unproven technology introduces risk.

- **Current workload.** Is this function currently overloaded with projects and this one adds to the burden? That's likely true of most functions, but if it's true, it needs to be discussed. Why is it happening?

- **Resources.** Are there enough resources, either in full-time employees (FTEs) or contractors, for the project?

- **Risks.** Are there any known risks from previous projects, upcoming events, or the project's environment? Consider threats and opportunities.

- **Issues.** Are there any impediments that might affect full performance? For example, a department might have just lost its leader or in some way been reshuffled. In a project that we mentioned earlier, the manager in the southeast United States was resistant because she was concerned that this project would be run almost immediately after a move and a reorganization. So we pushed the schedule out by a couple of months.

Break

The time after the functional presentations is a good time to take your first break. Not only does it give the attendees time to process what they've heard, it's a good place for a mental shift into the work of scoping the project. Additionally, breakout sessions could form as a result of deeper drill required on issues that may have been uncovered.

Breakout sessions should be encouraged, but not at the expense of the group working together on artifacts.

Assumptions

In order to proceed with any sort of project work, we must first list our assumptions. These assumptions can grow or shrink over the course of the project, and they're the precursors of risk. How many projects have failed because the team didn't consciously record and communicate their working assumptions? We know from our experience that the rate is over 50 percent. For example, if you're working on an international project and you make the assumption that the exchange rate between the involved countries is stable, there's a built-in threat that this exchange rate will change and cause issues with resources coming from a formerly low-cost country.

We need to be conscious of our assumptions and enumerate them. Let's look at what we mean by *assumption*: "A factor in the planning process that's considered to be true, real, or certain without proof of demonstration."

Understanding, and posting, our assumptions will act as a reality check against what we can and cannot due. For the sake of discussion, let's list some possible assumptions as we're going into the planning session:

- The architect will be available forty hours a week during the planning phase.

- The highest-quality building materials will be used.

- The project manager will work on no more than one project in addition to this one.

If you put the assumptions on a flip chart, it's entirely possible that someone may challenge them. For example, they might ask, "We need to control costs, does that come at a sacrifice to the quality of the house?" "If the project manager has to work on two projects simultaneously will it impact the schedule negatively?"

Make sure you connect the assumptions to the risk register. Each assumption is a "risk egg" waiting to hatch.

Constraints

Constraints are different from assumptions but are often mentioned in the same breath. Let's take a look at our Glossary definition: "A limiting factor that affects the execution of a project."

Why would we have constraints? Well, we always have them. Perhaps in the days of building the pyramids we had none. But in modern project management we have many limiting factors. For example:

- **Budget (cost).** If your budget for this project is $10M, then it can't simultaneously be $11M.

- **Schedule.** If the house is scheduled to be completed by August 31, then that is a limiting factor against which you must work.

- **Scope.** You're not building a twenty-room mansion; you're building a three-bedroom house.

As a matter of fact, those three items are classically called the Triple Constraint or the Iron Triangle. And in the best projects, these items – for every project – are ranked. So you might ask the sponsor which of these three is most important. If she says, for example, scope first, budget second, schedule third, then you have your marching orders.

Based on that, the house must be built exactly as designed, neither lesser than nor greater than the plan or design or blueprint. But if the schedule is third on the list, then that's the thing that could potentially slip. We're not saying that it should slip, just that that constraint, of the three, is the least constraining.

We've often seen the triple constraint with Quality added as a central feature (see Exhibit 9.2). One of us consulted to a manufacturing firm where Quality always won. That constraint was always more important than the other three. But the order of the other three might vary from project to project, depending on market conditions or even whether it's your flagship product or an R&D endeavor.

Another way to view the constraints is to go from the flat world of two dimensions to our world, which has at least three. So instead of a triangle, think of a pyramid. We describe this (we think, superior) constraint pyramid in our Refresher appendix. The main message is that scope, schedule, and cost are interdependent, and characteristics of the project's product (outcome) – the quality of the project – will put pressure on all three. Furthermore, risk – in the form of threat – will also challenge the constraints, in the form of, for example, installers showing up late, poor quality of workmanship, new scope being added to the project, or all of the above.

The Triple Constraint

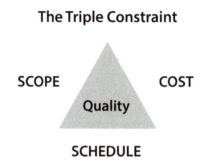

SCOPE   COST

Quality

SCHEDULE

Exhibit 9.2. Project professionals considering the triple constraint – scope, schedule, and cost – often add quality as a fourth constraint, and often consider it the most important one.

For the record, we're not saying that other companies allow quality to slip or be inferior. But sometimes, for example, software companies will allow a program with some minor bugs to be released with an eye toward fixing them in a subsequent release.

Everyone must leave this meeting with a solid understanding of the relative priority of these three constraints. They must know that, for example, time is of the essence (meaning that features may have to be reduced and/or the cost may have to go up).

Exhibit 9.3 shows an example from our case study in which we could use a constraint priority matrix to determine the ruling constraint. You'll want to make sure you capture the assumptions and constraints in an assumption log.

Estimating

Estimating is a task that everyone has to do and no one loves. That's because people are never really sure how long something will take. Five days? Ten days? In addition, they don't want to commit. If they tell you that an activity will take ten days and it actually takes fifteen, not only do they feel that they have let you down, they also feel that they're causing the project to be late.

Please note the connection between estimation and risk. We like to say that each estimate is an example of risk, by definition. "Five Days" may be three (an opportunity) or twelve (a threat). Each task length, or budget estimate, is only a single point from a future that we don't yet know. So estimation and risk are inexorably intertwined.

CONSTRAINT PRIORITY MATRIX				
	Enhance: **Top** **Priority**	Constrain: **Middle** **Priority**	Accept: Lowest Priority	**Comments**
Schedule		◆◆		A late project will not reflect well, so this is important but less so than budget.
Cost	◆◆◆			Given that Karyn will be judged on how she manages a budget, this is tops.
Scope			◆◆	If a feature or two must be sacrificed, that's not good, but something's got to give.

Exhibit 9.3. Constraint Priority Matrix: Everyone must leave the planning meeting understanding the relative priority of the three constraints.

In a perfect world, everyone would come to the meeting with historical data that details how long it takes to do a particular task. But that's in a perfect world. In the real world, outside of places like consulting firms and lawyers, who bill for their time, or the government, which uses time to track performance, relatively few people do this.

So when a developer is asked how long it should take to write a piece of code that he's written before, he'll often just blurt out a number. Not an uninformed number, mind you. But a number that in all likelihood has been padded to give himself extra time. This isn't necessarily a bad thing. We all do it. But at the end of the day, it isn't very scientific.

The Work Breakdown Structure

As mentioned in our Glossary, the work breakdown structure (WBS) is a task-oriented, detailed breakdown that defines the work packages and tasks at a level above that defined in the networks and schedules. This is a fundamental underpinning of project management planning that goes all the way back to the United States Department of Defense in the 1950s. To this day, the U.S. government still uses WBSs for all their projects, as do their government contractors.

The purpose of a WBS is to outline and visibly diagram the *what* of the work – in particular *what's in*, and, by its absence, *what's out*. Think of it as a hierarchical map of the project's scope. Each function will have a WBS, and it should detail what work needs to be done by each function.

It's very important to note, and for you to instruct, that the WBS is none of these:

- A timeline
- A bill of materials
- A budget
- A schedule
- A list of resources, or assignments to tasks

The WBS is the *enabler* of all those things, but it's *not* those things. It's important that the planning team, with you as the facilitator, focus the team on only the *what* and avoid getting hung up on duration, dependencies, assignments, costs . . . yet. When the WBS is complete, the team should be able to stand back and say, "That's what we need to do to complete our part of the project." That said, know this – the team will not instantly agree on how the WBS should be done or even exactly what's on it. That's okay! That's to be expected and is, in fact, part of the process.

Expect passion! Expect disagreements! Expect arguments! (But step in as needed.) The members of the team are having good and useful conversations. It's less important how they get there and more important that they get there at all. The team should understand that the WBS is subject to change. It's entirely possible that someone might have an ah-ha moment in the shower the next day and realize that they have to rework it to some degree.

Remember: if you fail to identify a chunk of work at this stage, it will not have:

- Resources assigned to it
- Assumptions collected for it
- Risks identified for it
- Money budgeted for it
- Schedule allocated for it

. . . and there may be dependencies on that chunk of work that are also left out. It could make your house into . . . a house of cards.

So it's a project imperative that the WBS be done and done properly.

Just to be clear, this isn't usually an exercise that the entire room does together. This is an exercise where each function, or workstream,

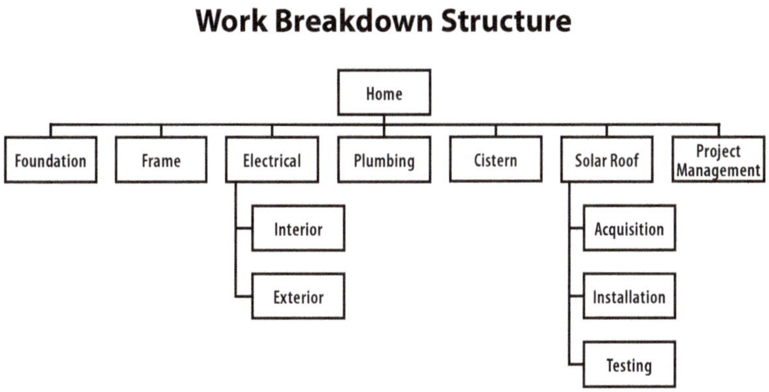

Work Breakdown Structure

Exhibit 9.4. A work breakdown structure is a hierarchical representation of the scope of the project. This is a simple WBS for building a sustainable house. For this illustration, we've broken down only two workstreams (Electrical and Solar Roof). In an actual project planning meeting, all workstreams should be broken down so that the work packages are visible.

prepares its own WBS. So in the case of Karyn's sustainably built house, we'll have a WBS for Framing, one for Plumbing, one for Electrical, etc. Visualizing it this way on the wall allows not only individual functions to see their work but also allows other functions to visit and comment. Later we'll link these workstreams.

Although there's an agreed-upon structure for the WBS, there's no one right way to do it. The key decision is at WBS Level 2. You can lay it out in a number of ways:

◆   By function

◆   By phases

◆   By deliverables

◆   By geographies

Whatever decision is made should be agreed-upon by all in the room. (We've chosen to use a functional model for this book.)

Exhibit 9.4 shows a WBS for Karyn's house project.

Step-by-step instructions for creating a WBS

Preparation: Each functional team should have a work area with enough wall space to accommodate several sheets of flip charts. They should

WBS for Electrical Function, One Level

| Electrical |

Exhibit 9.5. This and the following three exhibits represent the steps for creating the Electrical function's work breakdown structure for our case study. The very first item in the WBS is the name of the function – Electrical.

additionally have a generous supply of sticky notes in different shapes and colors.

Bear in mind that team members will not all be equally engaged. Typically in a team of, say, five, one or two will take the lead; some may hang back. Play to their strengths. Let them write on sticky notes, keep track of parking lot items, or review the WBS when it's complete.

Some will just naturally get it more quickly than others. You should reinforce the fact that the WBS is *not* a timeline. It's the what-we're-doing document, not the when, how, or who. Those will come later.

Here are the steps for creating the Electrical function's WBS for our case study:

1. Agree on a team lead, at least for this exercise. Anyone can write items down on sticky notes and affix them to the wall, but someone should facilitate this session. Some people will be shyer, less likely to lead the group or speak up. That's okay – let them contribute quietly in their own way. Sometimes these folks are great at looking at the whole picture and telling you what's missing.

2. Take a few sheets from the flip chart pad and affix them to the wall sideways – two or three should be sufficient.

3. The very first sticky note that goes up lists the name of the function – In this case it would be *Electrical*, which is Level 1 of the WBS (see Exhibit 9.5).

4. Level 2 of the WBS is where most of the controversy comes in. As mentioned earlier, you can do this by phases or by deliverables. However, it would be greatly advantageous if the project

WBS for Electrical Function, Two Levels

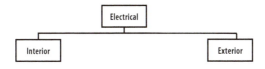

Exhibit 9.6. Choosing the items for Level 2 of the WBS can be controversial. You can use phases or deliverables. For our case study example we've chosen the two major phases.

manager and/or facilitator mandate what Level 2 should look like for all teams. A good practice is to find a somewhat analogous project that has done this before and work from their WBS – if your organization preserves such artifacts. (See Exhibit 9.6)

5. Level 3 of the WBS continues to break down the phases into more detail (see Exhibit 9.7).

6. From there, the team needs to brainstorm what comes next. As noted in the Glossary, a work package is defined as the lowest level of the WBS. So in this case, the team agrees that the lowest level will be an activity that goes no more than X amount of time. For example, 40 hours or perhaps two reporting periods for 80 hours.

7. Level 4 will now comprise all those components that make up Electrical: service panel, switches, set boxes, alarm sensors, HVAC. (This isn't meant to be a comprehensive list, just a

WBS for Electrical Function, Three Levels

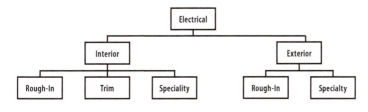

Exhibit 9.7. Level 3 breaks down the phases of Level 2 into more detail.

thought generator.)Typically you'll want to go at least three levels down. Remember the 100 percent rule, which states that the WBS includes 100 percent of the work defined by the project scope and captures all deliverables and activities – internal, external, interim – in terms of the work to be completed, including project management.

8. Your job is to go as many levels down as you need to – typically no more than three to five – to capture all the activities and deliverables that must be done in order to deliver all of the scope in a particular workstream (Electrical, Plumbing, or Carpentry).

9. As we mentioned, while creating a WBS seems like a relatively straightforward task, in reality teams will argue – no other word for it – over what needs to be done, even if they've done it before. And the more uncertain the project (as in R&D), the more challenging it is to accomplish. However, a great positive outcome of these arguments (if they're facilitated to focus on the issues and not the people, that is) is excellent buy-in to the result.

10. After the WBS is complete, teams should try to make a first-pass estimate of how long each work package will take to accomplish. Estimation is more art than science, but collectively they should make their best guesstimate based on experience. A technique we like, especially for activities that have greater uncertainty, is PERT (Program Evaluation Review Technique) three-point estimation in which you collect a Most Likely, a Pessimistic, and an Optimistic estimate. Give a weight of 4 to Most Likely, and use the equation:

     PERT Expected Value = [Pessimistic + (4 × Most Likely) + Optimistic] / 6

12. Now our WBS looks like what's shown in Exhibit 9.8.

13. Consider Exhibit 9.8 for a moment. Do all the Level 4 items add up to 100 percent of the house? Does something need to be added or subtracted? If so, keep working it until the WBS represents 100 percent of the house.

14. To demonstrate, let's just take Electrical and drill down further. What might one Level 4 item be? Electricians use a term called *rough-in*, which occurs after the framing goes in but before

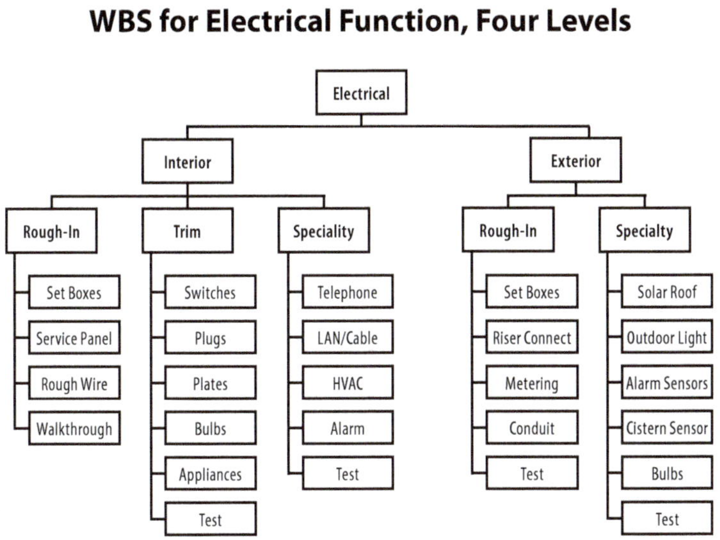

WBS for Electrical Function, Four Levels

Exhibit 9.8. Level 4 of the WBS comprises all of the components that make up Electrical.

drywall goes up. So it's the rough installation of wiring, boxes, breaker panel, etc.

15. Here are a few examples of items that might be in Level 4 (below Electrical) are:

   a. Set Electric Boxes

   b. Install Electric Service Panel

   c. Electrical Walk-through

   d. Electrical Rough-in

   Oops! Did we include cable TV and LAN wiring?

We put that exclamation here to remind you that you may discover, and should be seeking, new elements of work to include in the WBS. Don't fall into the trap of thinking that WBS completion is the same as project completion. Capture new work as it's discovered.

And so this exercise must be done for each item under Electrical until you've determined 100 percent of the work.

Teams will know that they're done when they can stand back, look at their WBS, and say to themselves, "That captures our work." That said, functional teams will want to visit each other to discuss their slice of the pie. Encourage this. Often this viewing, visiting, and reflection will cause a team to rethink their own WBS to some extent.

Typically, teams can finish the WBS by early-to-mid-afternoon of the first day. Regardless of when they finish, you should take a break, possibly a long one. Creating the WBS can be a rigorous exercise, especially for those who aren't used to doing it. A break gives teams time to reflect. You see that woman who's sitting there quietly staring at the WBS? Let her do it, don't break her thought. She's puzzling over something and will likely have a breakthrough, if history is any indicator.

After the break, each team should explain their piece of the puzzle – or rather, their branch of the WBS. This will give the entire group a chance to hear how each team sees its role in the project. Invariably, discussions will arise and WBS modifications may have to be made. This is perfectly okay – it's part of the buy-in that's so important to this exercise. Remind the team that the WBS is not yet set in stone. You're still very much engaged in planning, so items can be added or deleted as need be.

Schedule

If all goes well, the teams should be ready to develop the schedule immediately after discussing the WBS. Before you begin, it would be well to make sure the team understands the difference between a plan and a schedule, since many people have a tendency to conflate their meanings. (Note: If some teams are still working on their own WBSs, it's perfectly okay to start capturing information in the schedule. Overlap is acceptable.)

A plan is a formal written document typically explaining how you're going to do something; a schedule is a timeline. Very often in companies, project managers are asked to use Microsoft Excel as a scheduler. This is because it's already on everyone's desktop. We firmly believe that as a scheduler, Excel makes a very fine spreadsheet, but forcing it to make Gantt charts is just . . . wrong. In our opinion, a project manager working on an endeavor of any appreciable size and scope should be using a true project scheduler such as Microsoft Project, Oracle Primavera, or any of numerous online offerings such as ProjectManager.com.

The reason for this, in part, is that you can, and should, link all the project activities in a dynamic schedule. In this way, if an activity slips you can note that slippage in the schedule and it will push out accordingly. There's no such facility for this in Excel.

Additionally, true project schedulers have the ability to create different types of relationships between activities. If two activities can occur at the same time, but one activity must finish before the other one can finish, this can be manifested in the scheduler. This is a very common occurrence in the construction industry.

Whichever scheduler you choose, you should start the scheduling session by displaying a schedule on the screen. It doesn't have to be a real schedule from a real project, although if you have one, that might help. You are, as Stephen Covey says, beginning with the end in mind. You're showing your audience the goal that they're working towards.

Be advised: many team members, in the face of uncertainty, are reluctant to provide dates for completion of their activities; no matter how much you focus them on the activities, all they can see are dates. You need to help them separate activities from dates. For an example of this behavior from a real project, see our War Stories appendix.

Advise your teams that your goal for the session is to have a schedule displaying dependencies, dates, and milestones. Advise them further that you don't expect to have a finalized schedule by the end of two days, but rather a good first pass at a schedule. And that the work they did in creating the WBS will inform the schedule.

Let's stop here to review some terms:

- **Dependency.** A dependency is a relation between activities, such that one requires input from the other. Basically, what this means is that one activity depends on another. For example, when I go to paint my finished house (B), I cannot paint it until I buy the paint (A). So B depends on A.

  There are a variety of logical relationships, such as Start-Finish, Finish-Finish, Finnish-Danish, Swedish-Norwegian, and so on (we're kidding, of course; the four types are Finish-Start, Start-Start, Finish-Finish, and Start-Finish). We'll cover the real set of logical relationships a few paragraphs below. For now, we'll stick with what is by far the most common: Finish-Start. In the above example, buying paint must be *finished* before I can *start* the paint job.

73

♦ **Predecessor.** A predecessor is simply the task that must be finished before the next task can start. So, again leaning on our painting example, the purchase of paint is a predecessor to the paint job.

♦ **Milestone.** A milestone is a clearly identifiable point in a project or set of activities that commonly denotes a reporting requirement or completion of a key component of a project. For example, in the house-building project we might have this series of milestones:

  • Project begins

  • Permits received

  • Schedule developed

  • Foundation completed

  • Electrical work begins

As far as which milestones to make part of your schedule, that's very much up to you and your team. However, sometimes milestones are imposed, especially by management. If a company was releasing a product, and they wanted to demonstrate it at a trade show, there would a hard date for that show embedded in your schedule.

Let's say that your house WBS is now omplete. The next step is to get a connected picture – known as a network diagram – up on the wall. You might ask, "Why can't we just start entering the information into our scheduling software?" Strictly speaking, you could. But there's nothing more powerful than seeing an actual visual of the flow of the project. Also remember that "entering info into scheduling software" is an individual task in the WBS. And the WBS is much better if it's built by a team. Time spent having the entire team see the interconnections will lessen the time needed to enter those connections into your scheduler, and will make it much more likely that your entries are correct from the start. What you want to end up with is something like what's shown in Exhibit 9.9.

As you can see, this will assist you in visualizing the various interconnections. It may also assist you in estimating the duration of each activity, which is something you can record inside the various boxes (or nodes) as you progress.

So now the entire team is involved, figuring out which activity goes before which other activity, which milestones are important to show, and how all the pieces interconnect. But notice something important above. In every single case, the relationship between the activities is finish-to-start. In other words, before I start activity B, activity A must be completely done.

Well, ask yourself this question: Is that always the case? Are there some instances where two activities can start at the same time or finish at the same time? Are there activities that can run in parallel, saving you time?

The relationships between any two activities in the network diagram are called task dependencies, and their judicious use will help you to work more efficiently and effectively on your project. There are four types of task dependencies:

1. **Finish-to-start (FS).** I must finish Task A in order to start Task B. So if I'm building a house, I absolutely must have the frame of the house in place before I put the roof on. This is by far the most common task relationship type.

2. **Start-to-start (SS).** Start-to-start dependencies are used when the second task in the relationship can't begin until after the first task in the relationship begins. Start-to-start dependencies don't require that both tasks start at the same time.

   For example, Electrical Rough-in could start at the same time that Plumbing Rough-in starts. But we might introduce just enough lag (delay) so that the crews aren't bumping into each other.

3. **Finish-to-finish (FF).** If one of your tasks can't finish until another one finishes, you can use a finish-to-finish dependency between them. Finish-to-finish dependencies don't require that both tasks be completed simultaneously, they simply require that the first task be finished in order for the second task to finish.

   For example, let's say that the electrician is wiring a floor and will be followed by the person who installs the appliances. If we

Network Diagram

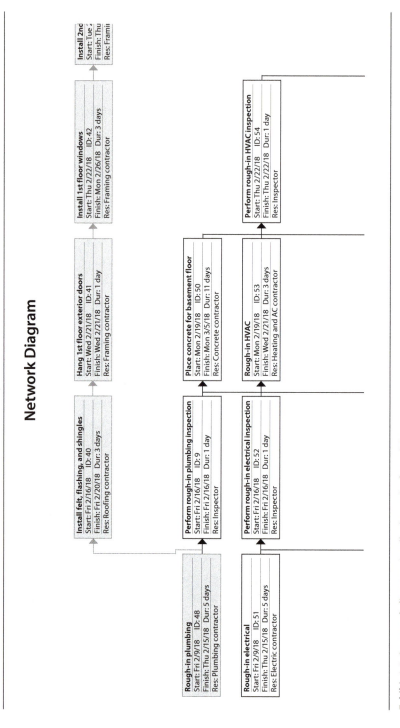

Install felt, flashing, and shingles
Start: Fri 2/16/18   ID: 40
Finish: Fri 2/20/18   Dur: 3 days
Res: Roofing contractor

Hang 1st floor exterior doors
Start: Wed 2/21/18   ID: 41
Finish: Wed 2/21/18   Dur: 1 day
Res: Framing contractor

Install 1st floor windows
Start: Thu 2/22/18   ID: 42
Finish: Mon 2/26/18   Dur: 3 days
Res: Framing contractor

Install 2nd
Start: Tue 2
Finish: Thu
Res: Frami

Perform rough-in plumbing inspection
Start: Fri 2/16/18   ID: 9
Finish: Fri 2/16/18   Dur: 1 day
Res: Inspector

Place concrete for basement floor
Start: Mon 2/19/18   ID: 50
Finish: Mon 3/5/18   Dur: 11 days
Res: Concrete contractor

Perform rough-in HVAC inspection
Start: Thu 2/22/18   ID: 54
Finish: Thu 2/22/18   Dur: 1 day
Res: Inspector

Perform rough-in electrical inspection
Start: Fri 2/16/18   ID: 52
Finish: Fri 2/16/18   Dur: 1 day
Res: Inspector

Rough-in HVAC
Start: Mon 2/19/18   ID: 53
Finish: Wed 2/21/18   Dur: 3 days
Res: Heating and AC contractor

Rough-in plumbing
Start: Fri 2/9/18   ID: 48
Finish: Thu 2/15/18   Dur: 5 days
Res: Plumbing contractor

Rough-in electrical
Start: Fri 2/9/18   ID: 51
Finish: Thu 2/15/18   Dur: 5 days
Res: Electric contractor

Exhibit 9.9. A network diagram visually shows the flow of the project.

make this relationship finish-to-start, it means that the appliance installer has to wait until the electrician is done.

But what if we make the relationship finish-to-finish? All that means is that the electrician must finish the wiring before the appliance person can plug everything in. Given that, does it matter whether the appliance person starts at the same time as the electrician? In theory, she could even place all the appliances in the room before the electrician even starts. All she has to do then is show up on the day the electrician finishes, plug everything in, and – done! This saves time, and in construction especially, FF dependencies are used all the time.

4.   **Start-to-finish (SF).** This is the rarest type of relationship and seldom used. The start-to-finish dependency is a little tricky. When you use this type of dependency, you are saying that the second task in the relationship can't finish until the first task starts. However, the second task can finish *any time* after the first task starts. Often this is used for shift work, such as that done by nurses, security guards, etc.

Your job now is to get that information into the schedule. Someone at this point will need to take ownership of the schedule, at least for the short term. Ideally that should be whoever the designated project manager is. However, we've been in situations where the project manager wasn't yet strong enough to lead this, so we as facilitators had to do it. We took a laptop and started entering the activities and dependencies from the network diagram into the scheduler. As we did this, we started to develop the first rough draft of a schedule.

As we mentioned earlier, the WBS is not meant to *be* the schedule – it's meant to illustrate the scope – to *be the basis* for the schedule. In fact, those of you who are already practicing project managers know that the WBS, in its outline form, is the left side of the Gantt chart, and the right-hand side with all of the pretty bars and arrows is simply the rendition of the time-phased execution of that scope.

Here are the steps for moving from the WBS to the schedule.

0.   **Look for missing pieces of work.** We make this Step 0 and not Step 1 intentionally. Start by reminding everyone that if it's not in the WBS it doesn't end up in the schedule. It's also true that

Don't Build a House of Cards

Exhibit 9.10. If your WBS is missing pieces of work, you may have just built a house of cards.

if it's not in the WBS, the work assignments, interdependencies, risks, costs, stakeholder relationships, in fact, all of the pieces of the project management infrastructure related to that missing piece, are also missing, and this jeopardizes the project execution. Think house of cards (see Exhibit 9.10).

So as you continue, look for missing pieces of work and add any that you find into the WBS. You're also looking to explicitly exclude scope that should *not* be part of your project.

1. **Put sticky notes in their proper sequence.** Work in functional sub-groups, and (of course after capturing the WBS with a smartphone photo) start to move the sticky notes around so that they're in the proper sequence. Each of the functional sub-groups are, for now, creating a "swim lane" for their function. If you have five functional groups, you'll temporarily have five functionally oriented network diagrams, based on that workstream from the WBS (see Exhibits 9.11 and 9.12). Don't worry – we intend to connect these with each other very soon.

WBS Workstream for Framing

Framing Workstream

House Building Project
1.1.1.1

Concrete 1.1.1	Framing 1.1.2	Plumbing 1.1.3	Electrical 1.1.4	Interior 1.1.5
Pour Foundation 1.1.1.1	Frame Exterior Walls 1.1.2.1	Instal Water Lines 1.1.3.1	Install Wiring 1.1.4.1	Install Drywall 1.1.5.1
Install Patio 1.1.1.2	Frame Interior Walls 1.1.2.2	Install Gas Lines 1.1.3.2	Install Outlets/ Switches 1.1.4.2	Install Carpets 1.1.5.2
Stairway 1.1.1.3	Install Roofing Trusses 1.1.2.3	Install Bath and Kitchen Fixtures 1.1.3.3	Install Fixtures 1.1.4.3	Painting 1.1.5.3

Exhibit 9.11. A WBS Workstream for Framing. Note that code of accounts numbering is shown. This is simply a scheme to show the indentedness of tasks – the longer the number, the deeper within a workstream one is. This is completely optional. Source: U.S. Department of Energy.

2. **Look for key milestones.** As you do this rearrangement of sticky notes, look for key milestones – zero duration project anchors such as "testing complete". By *zero duration* we mean that it's like a starting gun for a race, which, practically, takes no time, yet it's still an important event for the runners. Similarly, the crossing

Network Diagram for Framing

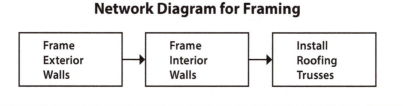

Exhibit 9.12. An elementary functional network diagram for framing based on the framing workstream from the WBS.

of the finish line takes no time, but clearly it's an important event for a race. Milestones in projects are often things such as "the end of the third quarter" or "achieving regulatory approval." To bring this home, for Karyn, literally, a very obvious milestone is the occupancy permit – not a task, but it's the attainment of that permit that allows her to move in (and make the home a part of her campaign). A trick we like is to use *square* (not rectangular) sticky notes and turn them 45 degrees to make a diamond. Diamonds represent milestones and are very important ways of checking for key deliverables (in this case, a test report). An additional tip: use a different color for milestones (if you were using yellow rectangular sticky notes for WBS items, use pink or blue for the milestones).

3. **Add the duration to the tasks.** If you haven't done so already, add the duration to the tasks. For example: run internal house wiring – seven days. You can use the PERT method we mentioned earlier to get an estimate more reflective of the uncertainty involved. Write this down on the sticky notes.

4. **Look for dependencies between tasks.** You can't frost a cake until it's baked, and you can't connect your outlets until the internal house wiring is completed. In those cases, "frost cake" has a dependency on "bake cake," and "connect outlets" has a dependency on "wiring completed." Look for these dependencies between tasks.

    Some tasks may have dependencies on two, three, or more other tasks (a merge), and some tasks may be a predecessor of two, three, or more other tasks (a burst). (See Example 9.13 for an example involving the framing of Karyn's house.) Indicate dependencies such as these with arrows. Tip: Use a whiteboard for the scheduling exercise, or you can use yarn and adhesive tape. Be creative.

    But make sure you understand which tasks (and milestones!) depend on the completion of which other tasks before they start. Note: For this stage of planning, assume all tasks to be finish-to-start, meaning that you must *finish* installing the house wiring

Task Dependencies for Framing

Example 9.13. This network diagram shows which tasks depend on the completion of which other tasks before they start. When more than one activity comes and joins an event (Framing), such an event is known as a merge event. When more than one activity leaves an event (Finalize Frame Design), such an event is known as a burst event.

before you *start* to connect the outlets, or as shown in Exhibit 9.13, you must finish training the framers before you begin framing.

5. **Look at how the different functional network diagrams connect.** This is a good time to have the teams rotate' – have the electrical team visit the framing team's work. You need to start looking at how each of these functional network diagrams connects with the others. For example, nobody is running any house wiring until the frame (or part of the frame, if you're working that way) is completed. At this point it's also a good idea, if you have the luxury, to invite project managers from analogous projects and/or technical subject matter experts to have a look at each of the individual functional groups' networks.

6. **Use project management software.** The facilitator should be using project management software (Microsoft Project, Primavera, Clarity, etc.) to begin entering information from all of the teams. Working from the WBS, the durations of the tasks, and the dependencies, project management software can calculate the critical path for the project – the longest path through the project (which indicates the shortest time in which the project can be completed). It will also be able to identify where there's slack or float – extra time available for a task.

We can potentially take resources from tasks with float and put them on critical paths in order to compress the schedule, but not without some risks. These risks include not taking into account learning curves and suffering from Brooks' law – where adding additional workers to a software project makes it later. For example, if the electrical work has significant float, these resources could work on framing – but not if they don't have the proper training and equipment to do so. Also, the framers may not want electrical dweebs stealing their work, and because they might have to train them, the critical framing task could take even longer to finish.

7. **Have a basis for your schedule.** When the intra-functional dependencies are logged, and the inter-functional dependencies have been considered, you have the basis for a schedule. It will now be a matter of the facilitator getting that (very drafty) Gantt-chart schedule circulated for review – but you have now generated a very thoughtful start to a schedule that has a much greater chance of:
   - Not leaving anything out that should be in scope
   - Excluding things that should be out of scope
   - Gaining strong buy-in from your team
   - Linking key deliverables to milestones and understanding the dependencies that lead to those milestone dates
   - Showing a realistic end-date, forecast not by a single person but by the group intelligence of your team.

End of Day One (Potentially)

It's impossible for us to predict where you'll leave off after the first day. But unless you have a very small project, or one that you've performed many times before, as likely as not you won't be finished with the schedule. The end of Day One is a good time to regroup, take a look at what the team has done, acknowledge and thank the team for that work, and set the stage for Day Two.

If the sponsor is available, she should come in and thank the team for their work. And as we mentioned when we talked about planning for the session, it's a great idea to have an outing for the team, some place where they can enjoy a dinner or bowling or something that keeps them engaged.

But there's typically some hard work left to do – someone has to finish recording as many of the sticky notes in the scheduler as possible. We have sometimes foregone the outing and stayed behind to work on the schedule. Failing that, someone (project manager, facilitator) should come in early the next morning and pull whatever level of schedule you have together, because it's important to show progress to the team.

It's a good idea to pull the team together at the end of the day and display the schedule on the screen. This is effective not only because they can see what a possible schedule might look like but also because they can see the fruits of their labor for the day. It will make the session feel that much more worthwhile.

Some people may ask you if they can have a copy to look at overnight. If so, tell them you'll send them a PDF that they can think about and mark up. These people are engaged, and you don't want to do anything to discourage that excitement.

Wrap Up Day One

Enough time should be left at the end of the day to quickly review what's been accomplished and what's still to be done. Review any parking lot issues and/or risk lists that may exist and discuss any open issues or side discussions that may have occurred. There should be no secrets, and all should be privy to decisions that potentially affect the outcome of the project.

If at all possible, the sponsor should give a talk at day's end and gather feedback that would help improve the next day's session.

Party

If you've arranged some sort of first-night get together, make sure you hand out a note summarizing all the arrangements. Tell people that you don't want to talk business at night; you want them to have fun.

Day Two

Once Day Two begins, and after everyone has recounted stories about what a wild man Bob is when he's out on the town, you should display the draft schedule on the screen. There won't necessarily be any *oohing* and *aahing*, but people will certainly appreciate seeing the schedule where yesterday they had literally nothing.

So what exactly do you do on Day Two? Well, frankly, for quite a bit of the day you'll be continuing to work on the schedule. The project manager will visit each team to discuss how to link together dependencies and will enter those into the schedule. But overnight, magically, the teams will have thought of more things. And so you'll have to add those. Since the project manager can visit only one team at a time, the other teams can be thinking about their dependencies, adding or subtracting activities, etc.

What you don't want is people casually sitting around talking and drinking coffee as if they think they're "done." *Challenge* them. See if they've really thought everything through. If they have, see if they can assist other teams. Also, certain technical or organizational issues have likely cropped up. Now is the time to get sidebar discussions going, where these issues can be worked on. Because, in all likelihood, you'll rarely if ever get this team together again in this way.

You will also want to get the teams started working on risk. Eventually everyone will finish their schedule piece and resolve or table technical issues. So now, inevitably, you'll need to start dealing with risk.

What typically happens during this first part of Day Two is that some groups are thinking through their dependencies, others are excusing themselves for a "moment" and making phone calls, some are looking at risk, and others are in break-out sessions discussing technical or marketing or product issues that have surfaced as a result of the meeting.

Your job as facilitator is to help attendees think through their parts of the schedule. Does activity A really come before activity B? Do both activities A and B have to happen before C does? Can some of these activities be finish-to-finish? Start-to-start?

This is where some intense group discussion occurs. Often teams get creative and rethink the process. "Well," they'll say on thinking about it. "Maybe we could run those processes in parallel and shave a few days off the schedule." Encourage this kind of creative, open-ended thinking, but make sure that the teams understand the trade-offs. If work is done in parallel are there going to be some threats introduced? Identify them now, and review them in a meeting focused specifically on risk identification.

Also, teams should have estimated the duration of activities during the creation of the WBS, but there's no reason not to rethink those. In fact, it's very likely that, under discussion, not only will new activities surface, but durations of already existing ones will be changed. Again, this is a planning session, a sandbox, if you will, so nothing is cast in stone.

Risk Analysis and Identification

One of your key jobs as a project manager – which translates to a specific function as a facilitator – is for you and your team to initially, and continually, identify risk on the project. The continually part is important – yes, it has to be done at the start of the project, but risk is dynamic, and so are your risk responses. By *response* we mean what you're actually going to do to deal with the risk should it occur. There's a chance that your responses have residual (leftover) risks and cause new (secondary) threats to occur. These will be discussed in detail a bit later in this section. All of this activity has to be monitored and controlled by the team with your guidance.

To recap, by now you've created your functional WBSs and you have a good initial draft schedule. It's time now to figure out what your risks are. As per the Glossary, *risk* is defined as "an uncertain event, which, if it occurs, has a positive or negative effect on one or more project objectives." A risk is something that *may* happen, not something that *will* happen. The latter is a fact – perhaps an issue. If Jane is going on maternity leave, that's a fact. Her absence is, however, a risk to your project's objectives, which means that you'll either have to postpone the project or find another resource.

So it's important to determine what the threats are to your project, and it's also important to identify the possible things that could go horribly right. (We call those opportunities.) The good news is that we now have an excellent idea of what our activities are, and with those and the WBS, we can now start to look at risks. In fact, you may well have put some risks on your parking lot flip chart while you were doing your previous work.

Let's make sure that we can differentiate a risk from its cause and its effect. These are commonly confused, so let's de-confuse them. The cause-risk-effect method of analyzing risk is well-established and helps you not only to isolate the real risk but also, in some cases, to determine the root cause. For example:

Because I'm using retread tires, there's a *risk* of getting a flat tire, which might have the *effect* of my having an accident. The tires aren't the risk nor is the accident; the risk is getting a flat tire. So if it helps your team to parse it this way, do so. Your risk register doesn't necessarily have to show all three, but it couldn't hurt.

Let's take a moment to clarify risks versus issues. A risk *may* happen; an issue *has* happened. If the risk occurs, it's now an issue and must be owned and dealt with. Of course, it's possible that an issue just crops up and was never an identified risk to begin with.

But let's get back to the first pass at risk identification, near the start of your planning meeting. You want to engage your team and make sure that they're ready to look broadly and deeply for all sorts of things that could go wrong. You'll want to have them avoid the bias in some cultures (American, for example), where identifying threats can cause someone to be labeled a naysayer. Of course, you really, really want these naysayers at this point in the project meeting because you want to deeply explore the project for risks so that you have a chance to respond to them. Make sure you consider these particular sources of threats:

- Assumptions you've made; each assumption is a larval risk. For example: Vendor ABC will perform exactly as they say in their brochure, or they'll perform exactly as they did last time.

- Estimates (estimate *ranges* can yield threats, opportunities, and even drivers/causes of threat). For example: Permit XYZ takes anywhere from three to six weeks to obtain, depending on whether or not we have a pre-inspection. The wider the range, the riskier this assumption.

- Lessons learned from previous, similar projects. For example: Last time we built one of these houses, the solar panels took three extra weeks to arrive due to a customs inspection issue.

You should guide your team through these considerations.

Once your risks are identified, they go into an ever-evolving and constantly updated risk register. In the register, the risks are clearly explained, including what their impact will be on the project, and a first pass at a risk response. A risk register is commonly manifested in a spreadsheet and typically looks something like what's shown in Exhibit 9.14.

RISK REGISTER

Risk	Risk Category	Probability	Impact	Risk Score	Risk Ranking	Risk Response	Trigger	Risk Owner
Due to a shortage in the market, solar panels may not arrive on time causing a delay to the end date	Materials	8	9	72	1	Save LEED install to end of project	Business news indicates that solar manufacturers are back ordered.	Environmental SME
Due to schedule conflicts, the architect may be unavailable for one month in spring causing a delay to the end date	...	...	...	...	...	...	...	...
...	...	...	...	...	...	...	...	...
...	...	...	...	...	...	...	...	...
...	...	...	...	...	...	...	...	...
...	...	...	...	...	...	...	...	...

KEY TERMS

Risk: The risk stated in a complete sentence hat states the cause of the risk, the risk, and the effect that the risk causes to the project.

Risk Category: Categorization of risks by area of project affected, source of risk, or other useful category.

Probability: The likelihood that a risk or opportunity will occur (on a scale from 0 to 10 with 10 being the highest).

Impact: The impact of the risk on the project if the risk occurs (scale from 0 to 10 with 10 being the highest).

Risk Score: Determined by multiplying probability and impact (scale from 0 to 100).

Risk Ranking: A priority list that's determined by the relative ranking of risks (by their scores) to the project with number one being the highest risk score.

Risk Response: The action that's to be taken if this risk occurs.

Trigger: Something that indicates that a risk is about to occur or has already occurred.

Risk Owner: The person who the project manager assigns to watch for triggers and manage the risk response if the risk occurs.

Exhibit 9.14. A risk register is commonly created in a spreadsheet and typically looks like this partially filled register.

Probability/Impact Matrix (Heat Map)

Probability (Likelihood)	Very Low	Low	Medium	High	Very High
Very High	P: Very High I: Very Low	P: Very High I: Low	P: Very High I: Medium	P: Very High I: High	P: Very High I: Very High
High	P: High I: Very Low	P: High I: Low	P: High I: Medium	P: High I: High	P: High I: Very High
Medium	P: Medium I: Very Low	P: Medium I: Low	P: Medium I: Medium	P: Medium I: High	P: Medium I: Very High
Low	P: Low I: Very Low	P: Low I: Low	P: Low I: Medium	P: Low I: High	P: Low I: Very High
Very Low	P: Very Low I: Very Low	P: Very Low I: Low	P: Very Low I: Medium	P: Very Low I: High	P: Very Low I: Very High

Impact (Consequence): Very Low · Low · Medium · High · Very High

Exhibit 9.15. A probability and impact (or PI) matrix is usually colorized so that the northeast corner is red and the southwest corner is green, with commensurate shading of yellows in between to indicate that high combinations of probability and impact (for threats) are worthy of escalation (they're red) and threats that have combinations of low impact and/or low probability don't need as much attention (they're green). In this exhibit we use shadings to represent the colors, with dark gray representing red and white representing green. The downloadable template (see Appendix F) will show colors.

But how do we get to that end result? Well, since risk is measured in terms of probability and impact, the first thing you'll want to do is create what we call a probability and impact matrix (some call it a heat map) on a flip chart on the wall as shown in Exhibit 9.15.

A heat map is simply a form of probability and impact (or PI) matrix that has been colorized so that the northeast corner is red and the southwest corner is green, with commensurate shading of yellows in

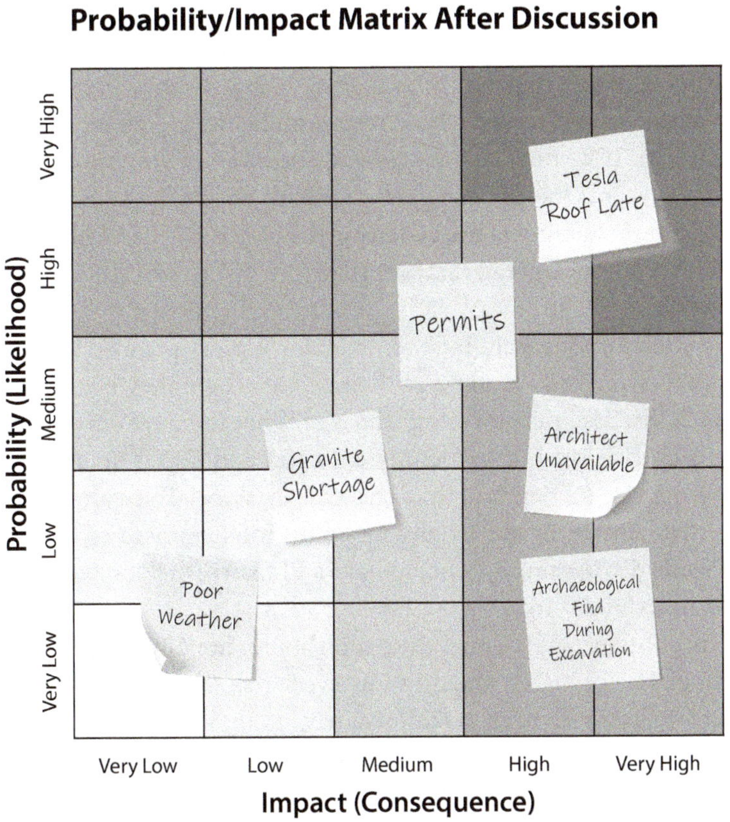

Probability/Impact Matrix After Discussion

Exhibit 9.16. You and your team write possible threats on sticky notes and then decide where they belong on the probability/impact matrix. Move the sticky notes around based on the judgment of the group. After some discussion, you should have a matrix that looks like the one above.

between to indicate that high combinations of probability and impact (for threats) are worthy of escalation (they're red) and threats that have combinations of low impact and/or low probability don't need as much attention (they're green). Exhibit 9.16 shows an example of a heat map from our house-building case study.

You can see that the goal is to take every single risk identified and decide on its probability of occurring and its impact if it does. And clearly, the ones in the upper right quadrant will be of much greater concern than those in the lower left.

89

You might wonder if the decision about impact or probability is somehow scientifically decided. In fact, it's not. It's somewhat subjective. But to use our home-building analogy as an example, imagine that a risk is that solar panels may not be available. Who determines that risk? As likely as not it's the person whose responsibility it is to either acquire or install them. If he does this for a living, are we not going to trust him when he says that there's been a shortage of them and he believes that the impact and probability of not acquiring the panels is high? And won't his opinion be of much greater import than that of the proverbial man-on-the-street?

So you and your team have to write down every possible threat they can think of on sticky notes and then decide where they belong on the PI matrix. This is brainstorming. The idea is not to figure out what to do about each risk but just to identify each risk and slap it up somewhere on the matrix. Remember, this isn't cast in stone. You can use sticky notes that can be moved around based on the judgment of the group. After some discussion, you should have a PI matrix that looks like what's shown in Exhibit 9.16.

Once the matrix is done, the team should, literally, stand back and look at it. The PI matrix should show every risk they can think of, with probabilities and impacts. (Okay, you have to draw the line somewhere. An asteroid hitting a manufacturing plant is a possibility, but unless you see that as a real threat, keep it (and those types of unlikely risks) off your matrix. On the other hand, the possibility of a hurricane in Florida, or a nor'easter in New England, is very real.)

Now that you've come up with your list of prioritized risks, the next step is to put them into a ranked risk register. There's no particular tool that must be used to store your list of risks, but spreadsheets lend themselves quite well to this. Our template can assist you (see Appendix F).

What you'll want to do is simple – put the risks in the register in ranked order based on your PI results. When it's done it should look something like what's shown in Exhibit 9.17.

Risk Response

The question now becomes what to do about those risks. Certainly you'll want to focus heavily on the ones at the top of your ranking, and perhaps some of the medium-level ones. (The Project Management Institute

				RISK REGISTER SHOWING PRIORITIZED RISK RANKING				
Risk	Risk Category	Probability	Impact	Risk Score	Risk Ranking	Risk Response	Trigger	Risk Owner
Due to a shortage in the market, solar panels may not arrive on time causing a delay to the end date	Materials	8	9	72	1	Save LEED install to end of project	Business news indicates that solar manufacturers are back ordered.	Environmental SME
Due to schedule conflicts, the architect may be unavailable for one month in spring causing a delay to the end date	Resource	7	6	42	2	Move design to earlier in project	Comment about "being to busy for this" from architect overheard by electricial	Project Manager
Due to granite being imported from India, it might not arrive on time for the kitchen install causing a delay to the end date	Materials	5	7	35	3	Look for another source; consider domestic granite	News reports indicate Indian granite is becoming harder to adquire	Project Manager
Because builders may not have enough experience with green/LEED sites, it may take longer to construct the house	Resource	4	6	24	4	Training	Review of LEED construction guidelines indicates more sophisticated construction techniques will be used	Environmental SME
Due to possible conflicts between federal and local green regulations, there may be significant delay in implementation	Regulatory	4	5	20	5	Assign interns to research the possible conflicts between these regulations in advance	Initial reports from interns	Environmental SME
Due to a shortage in the market, solar panels may be more expensive causing a change to the cost baseline	Cost	4	5	20	6	Assure high priority with Tesla, not that this is a showcase building for a political campaign	Notice on Tesla website indicating potential sourcing problems	Environmental SME

Exhibit 9.17. Ranked risk register with risks ranked based on PI results. In addition to risk scores, risks rankings are usually shown in colors (red for high risk, yellow for moderate risk, and green for low risk). In this exhibit we use shading to represent risk ankings (dark for high risk, moderate for moderate risk, and light for low risk).See Exhibit 9.15 for definitions of terms. The downloadable template (see Appendix F) will show colors.

suggests that you put the lower-ranked ones on a watch list because those can easily bubble up if left unwatched and become major risks.)

For threats, we can respond in the following five ways:

- **Escalate.** This response is for those threats that are outside the scope of the project or that require greater authority than that granted to the project manager. For example: While digging the trough for the cistern, remains of a Kumeyaay Indian settlement are discovered. The project manager contacts Karyn, who in turn must escalate to determine next steps.

- **Accept.** Let it happen, either without doing anything (passive acceptance) or with some form of contingency plan (active acceptance). For example: The manufacturer of the cistern system reports that it may only collect 85 percent of the water originally advertised. It's still saving water, so just accept this fact.

- **Mitigate.** Try to change the probability of the threat, and/or the impact of the threat if it does occur. For example: Exceedingly hot days are forecast for the region. Be sure to have cooling fans and cold water to mitigate heat exhaustion for the construction staff.

- **Avoid.** Change the plan to not even deal with that threat. Normally when we avoid, we're also avoiding some benefit. For example: The Tesla roof price looks like it's going to double. Go to a standard roof with solar panels.

- **Transfer.** Give the threat to someone else – usually for a large fee. For example: The Tesla roof installation can't be done by Karyn's preferred roofing company, so it's outsourced to a specialty company that has had proven success with Tesla roofing tiles.

For opportunities, there are also five ways to respond (Escalate and Accept are common to both threats and opportunities):

- **Escalate.** This response is for those opportunities outside the scope of the project or that require greater authority than that granted to the project manager. For example: While digging the trough for the cistern, gold flecks are found, indicating a possibly rich vein of gold ore in the area. Karyn must be alerted to this possible source of campaign funding.

- ◆ **Accept.** Let it happen, either without doing anything (passive acceptance) or with some form of contingency plan (active acceptance). For example: The electrical subcontractor is performing at a tremendous pace and may finish three days early.

- ◆ **Enhance.** Try to increase the probability of the opportunity and/ or increase the positive impact of the opportunity if it does occur. For example: The site supervisor notices that the framing workers do better when they're listening to music. Notified of this, you provide a wireless music system and earbuds to the framers.

- ◆ **Exploit.** Change the plan to try to assure that this opportunity happens. For example: Tesla is offering a discount if Karyn's house will put up a Tesla Roofing sign in front of the project worksite. She accepts this and gets 10 percent off her price.

- ◆ **Share.** Partner with a specialist to get the most out of the opportunity. For example: Back to our gold example, Karyn teams with a company that specializes in small mining operations.

You'll work with your team to brainstorm the proper type of response, and the specific action to implement that response, for each risk in the risk register.

There are also overall project risks and Avoid, Exploit, Transfer, Share, Mitigate, Enhance, and Accept responses still apply. Think of overall project risk as those risks that over-arch the entire project. If, for example, your project is to ship a delicate package on a large seagoing vessel to another continent, you would identify risks such as poor packaging of the item in a box, careful transport of the box from your location to the ship's dock, and so on. However, if your box is being shipped via the HMS *Titanic*, there's an overall project threat, called "The Titanic Sinks." This is represented very well in a one-minute video that you can find at bit.ly/titanicsinks.

In our case study, an earthquake in Karyn's worksite area would be an example of an overall project risk.

As your project develops, you should be using the risk register as the repository for risks, risk owners, and risk responses. This will be fundamental to the Lessons Learned effort for the project.

A risk owner is someone who "owns" the risk on your behalf during the life of the project. You, as PM, own the risk register. But someone, say a team member, would monitor specific risks and perform mitigations if and/as needed. In our example, the environmental SME might own any energy-related risks

Risk will change and fluctuate throughout the project. Some risks will be closed; others will have their priority and/or impact go up or down. It is a living document and so when you change a risk, it may go from low to medium to high. (Or hopefully, the reverse.)

When you modify the cell contents, it's an easy matter to change a cell to red, yellow, or green depending on a formula that reflects its contents. Our template will do that for you.

Once you have the register, you'll have to decide what to do about each risk, since each one requires a response. (You may not have time to fully flesh this out in the meeting, but you can make a good start.)

Recall that earlier we introduced the concepts of secondary and residual risk. Here's an example of each:

- **Secondary risk.** Look *up*. Yes, we mean it. Right now, look straight above you. If you're sitting in an office, you'll probably see a sprinkler head of some sort – a small device hanging from the ceiling, resembling a ninja star, or a snowflake. That sprinkler head is a form of risk response for the threat of fire. If you aren't in an office, we're sure you've seen these devices before. In any case, if fire is detected, that sprinkler head will spray water to extinguish the fire. Now, look *down*. Imagine that beneath you is a server farm with US$40M worth of equipment and tons of proprietary information. The water from the sprinkler system has to go somewhere – and it has drenched and ruined the server farm. That is secondary risk.

- **Residual risk.** Imagine again that the sprinkler system is activated due to a fire, and the installation was poor, or water pressure is low, so the sprinklers do not extinguish the fire, or do not extinguish it quickly enough. That is risk which remains after the response – or residual risk.

94

Exhibit 9.18. Working session for creating a work breakdown structure.

Closing the Planning Meeting

You've reached the end of the planning meeting. The walls are full of flip charts, sticky notes and scrawled, handwritten notes. The tables have half-full cups of coffee and soda (and in the old days, cigarettes). Everyone has been hard at work for two or more days and they're somewhat dazed and confused.

What now? Well, time to regroup and pull the whole thing together. If the sponsor hasn't been present for the entire meeting, this is a good time for her to return. She should discuss the project with the team as a group, including any findings, risks, and issues. Be prepared to take notes since the team's understanding of the project should be significantly increased over what it was just two days ago. You've been on a journey.

But, as in any other project, it's not the best practice to just walk away. You don't want to have done all this hard work only to have everyone wondering what to do next. There should be some clear steps taken.

The sponsor, after discussing the project with the team, should take time to thank everyone for coming and acknowledge the hard work that's been done. She should also say that this will be a standard methodology for any project going forward or, at least, any large, multifunctional project.

This is also a good time for the sponsor to ask if there are any last-minute things anyone wants to say while the group is assembled. Often the observations made post-meeting are quite insightful. She should also solicit feedback from the group as to whether the exercise was worth their time. Our observation is that in a well-run facilitation, the answer is typically yes. That said, it doesn't hurt to do a brief lessons learned. You'll often hear things like "I wish we'd spent more time on the risk register" or "We should have done more pre-work." The project manager should capture these thoughts for the next facilitation.

The project manager should make sure that all issues and risks are understood by the team. Issues, with dates for resolution, should be assigned to team members. Risks should have responses and risk owners. The project manager should also advise the team that he'll be visiting with them in the near future to finalize the schedule (remember that this is only a first draft) and will be producing and posting a risk/issue register.

As much as possible – and this is key – the project manager will state dates for when these things will occur, and he'll circulate them later by email. Follow-up on these items is crucial, otherwise it will seem to everyone that they had a few nice days out of the office and the meeting was just like every other one they've been to.

People will want to take their WBSs with them. You can tape the sticky notes to the flip charts and roll them up to take them back. And, of course, everyone takes pictures of everything with their phones these days.

Paul Axtel (2015), in a recent *Harvard Business Review* article, says:

> In my 35 years of experience as a corporate trainer, I've found that closure is more often than not the missing link between meetings and impact. Without it, things can be left unsaid, unchallenged, unclear, and/or uncommitted. Each agenda item should be considered incomplete unless it is wrapped up in a thoughtful, deliberate way.

Axtel goes on to provide a simple, five-step process for the end of the meeting:

1. Check for completion.
2. Check for alignment.
3. Agree on next steps.
4. Reflect on the value of what you accomplished.
5. Check for acknowledgements.

We agree. We think that closing a meeting is critical, and if it's skipped, or done poorly, it's worse than if the meeting hadn't taken place at all. Because not only did you not get what you needed from the meeting, you've wasted the valuable time of your project team members and other stakeholders, and, more damagingly, established a precedent for folks to believe that your meetings aren't worth their time in the future.

What's important to note here, and it's something we've threaded throughout the book, is that, just as in project management itself, the setup for a successful closing isn't just the closing itself. It's the way in which the meeting is run that allows the meeting to close properly, and allows you as the facilitator to properly perform the steps above.

To that end (excuse the pun), we've drawn from an article by Peter Economy (2016) called "7 Ways to End Every Meeting on a Positive Note." His article reflects our philosophy that the ending of the meeting is a result, not of the things you do at the very end, but of what you do *before* and *during* the meeting. We've taken each of those seven ways and added our take from a project meeting perspective:

1. **Don't let it drag on.** Have a timer (one of those little hourglass things can work, or use a feature on your smartphone) to alert you when there are ten minutes left to the meeting. Use that as your trigger to make sure you can wrap up on time. If there are heavy issues that would take longer, don't let the meeting keep going – take a note of those issues and dedicate a new meeting to them. Don't try to rush those through in the last thirty-seven seconds.

2. **Keep it positive.** Find the good in the meeting and be sure to wrap up by acknowledging the (hopefully many) agreements, next steps, and decisions that were accomplished in the meeting.

3. **Be nice – like you mean it!** This is simply about warmly acknowledging everyone who came and thanking them earnestly for their time at the meeting.

4. **Neutralize a touchy meeting.** If there have been heated discussions and controversy, and you sense that there have been hurt feelings, acknowledge this, and indicate how you'll deal with this on an ongoing basis. Or at least indicate that you plan to determine how to do this as a priority action as the project manager.

5. **Redirect a pointless meeting.** If the project meeting is heading off into non-productive tangents, STOP! Ask your team members to take a couple of minutes on their own to jot down the items they feel need further consideration, and arrange one-on-one meetings with them to help tailor the next meeting. Now you can get on with the planned project agenda.

6. **Open up the meeting.** Save five to ten minutes at the end of each meeting to give all team members an opportunity to add a comment and have their say *without interruptions* – this is their time to speak.

7. **End it with action!**

Review the action items and next steps. Remind attendees of how the meeting's results help the project and how the project helps the organization. End with enthusiasm!

Follow-Up

Using your existing issue log and other project tools, you need to track action items from project meetings. But you also should take a moment at the start of each meeting to review the progress on meeting-sourced action items; this gives the team members a sense of progress and lets them know that action items aren't theoretical or imaginary things, but actual tasks that must be done in support of the project objectives.

CHAPTER TEN

Facilitating a Virtual Meeting

Wayne Turmel

Here's everything you need to know about virtual kickoff meetings: they're kickoff meetings that happen to be held virtually. I'm not being facetious, here. It's critical that we keep first purposes in mind. They're kickoff meetings first and foremost.

Too often we get hung up on the "virtual" piece. Worrying about the webcam or audio problems, or wondering if the people who aren't in the conference room with you are paying attention, answering email, or getting to the next level on Minesweeper, can cause a lot of stress and problems that interfere with your team's goals for the project.

There's a statistic I like to share with people in our classes. It has two parts:

- Two thirds of the time spent on virtual meetings (web meetings, videoconferences, teleconferences) is considered wasted by attendees. But . . .

- The time considered wasted on "real" meetings is still 50 percent or more.

In other words, meetings pretty much suck. Making them virtual just adds a bit to the general suckiness. There is some good news, though. Just as with proper planning, preparation, and facilitation your regular meetings can be more effective, the same is true with virtual meetings.

And it really doesn't matter what tools or platforms you use, as long as you use them effectively. Remember, Genghis Khan ruled half the known world and never held a single conference call.

The trick is to plan your meeting first, and then use the technology (as well as you can) to eliminate, mitigate, or at least do the best you can to overcome any challenges posed by distance.

So, you need to think about your meetings in the following order:

- What are you trying to accomplish? What do you want participants to do/contribute/walk away with?

- What tools are at your disposal to accomplish these goals?

- What do you need to do as the meeting leader before, during, and after the meeting, then to ensure success?

You won't be surprised to see that these are the exact same things we (should) consider before any meeting.

What Are You Trying to Accomplish?

If form follows function, then you have to start with the simple question, "What am I trying to accomplish?" Any good project kickoff has the same components. You want to deliver information in a way that's easily understood, answer questions, and help the team form (if they don't already know each other). You also want to allow for questions so that not only does everyone understand their roles, goals, and duties, but you have a reasonable amount of faith that they get it.

So what should you do to accomplish that? You need a way to transmit information in as many ways as possible (visual, verbal, vocal), and receive feedback in as many ways as possible. Now, how will you accomplish that in a virtual environment?

Understanding the Tools at Your Disposal

We said earlier that kickoff meetings are, first and foremost, just meetings that are held virtually. Technology is merely another constraint among many you'll face on your project. The good news is that you probably have, or have access to, most of the tools you'll need. The bad news is you may not know it.

This isn't a surprise. Eighty percent of people who use tools such as Skype for Business or WebEx use only 20 percent of the features. In project work that's fairly surprising, given that we tend to be tech- and process-oriented people to start with. Still, we're human and tend to use only as much of a given technology as we think we need to get the job done.

Part of the problem is that over 70 percent of users use these tools for the first time in front of live victims. We don't get any training or coaching on the presentation platform other than how to fire it up and do the bare minimum. We've never seen most of the tools used in the context of a good meeting, so we don't think about applying them in a broader way.

At first this seems counter-intuitive. The approximately 120 web-meeting and presentation platforms out there are all approximately the same in terms of functionality. The best analogy is renting a car. You may not know how the headlights turn on for a particular model, but you're pretty sure that the car has them, and you just need to know where the darned button is.

We also need to acknowledge that there are three types of meetings, and they each have their own challenges. First is the traditional, in-person meeting, where everyone's in the same room at the same time. We have a lifetime of experience with these, which doesn't mean that we're good at them, but at least we have the advantage of being all together at the same time, getting the messages unfiltered, and having free communication.

Next is the totally virtual meeting. We're limited by the platform we're using, but at least in a virtual meeting everyone is on WebEx, or Skype, and has equal access to the platform and, in the right hands, an equal ability to take part. Nobody has an advantage over anyone else; we're all equally miserable.

Finally, there's the hybrid meeting. If you've ever been in a meeting where some people are in the conference room, and the rest are connected to a squawky speaker phone, and there's a tangible power imbalance as a result, you're familiar with hybrid meetings. Some people are having an in-person experience, others are at the mercy of technology and a lack of visibility. Ignore the very real dynamics at your peril.

But since we're letting form follow function, let's put this whole technology discussion into context – what are you trying to do, and how can the tools help or hinder your effectiveness?

What's the Function that Form Follows?

If we quickly list the things that need to happen for any meeting to be successful, you'll see that it doesn't matter much whether the meeting is online or in Conference Room B. There are multiple ways to achieve each goal. The trick, if we're working virtually, is to find the best feature or function that allows us to achieve that goal as effectively as possible.

For example, when I ask people, "What would you do in a face-to-face meeting to get input?" they might say something like, "Ask for a show of hands." In a conference room, everyone knows to raise their hand. Did you know that most virtual meeting platforms have a "raise hand" feature? That's a tool that levels the playing field, but if you don't know about it you can't utilize it.

So, as the kickoff meeting facilitator, what are you trying to do?

- Help everyone on the team get to know the leaders, stakeholders, and each other.

- Deliver information in a multitude of ways and media so that people really understand what the project is (the big picture) and their role in it (individual roles and tasks).

- Answer any questions or objections people may have.

- Collaborate to create processes, team norms, and action items.

- Ensure understanding and buy-in.

- Leave people feeling energized, positive, and with some of their will to live intact.

Helping Everyone Get to Know Each Other

Everyone knows that a team is only as good as the working relationships between its members. The kickoff is often the first, and often one of the few, opportunities for everyone to get to know who they're working with. We need to have as full an experience of each other as possible. That means visual, vocal, and verbal communication. If the team in Bangalore is simply a list of names to the team in Boston, you're beginning the working relationship at a disadvantage.

In a traditional meeting you can go around the room and have everyone introduce themselves. You can see each other, hear one another, joke, laugh, and get to know one another. In a virtual meeting you have the opportunity to use webcams and other ways for people to interact. And in hybrid meetings everyone may or may not be able to make an equally good first impression.

Here are some of the tools, and tips for using them, that will help. Most virtual meeting platforms will allow you to do some version of these.

- **See each other.** Our brains crave visual connection. The most powerful way of introducing people to each other is to make sure that they connect a face with a voice and a role. In person this happens automatically. Online, you need to take advantage of webcams and video conferencing. It doesn't have to be high-tech Cisco Telepresence (although that's a lovely tool). A simple webcam (assuming you can actually see the person and they aren't backlit like they're in Witness Protection) will do. If that's impossible, at least have photographs of participants that you can share with the team.

  Use webcams. If you're doing the meeting totally online, encourage everyone to use their webcams, at least for introductions. If you're having a hybrid meeting, try projecting the web meeting (using something like WebEx) so that people will be able to at least see the webcam images of the remote team members.

- **Hear each other.** One very common mistake people make is to automatically mute everyone who isn't in the room. (And let's face it, it's the ones in the room who need muting, more often than not.) This sends the message that anyone remote is less important than everyone else, and you'll have to work harder to get them to contribute, because they've essentially been told to shut up and not speak unless spoken to. If at all possible, allow them the choice of muting themselves or not. Be very clear that their input is wanted, and that they can unmute themselves at will. If they have background issues (barking dogs, crying co-workers) they can turn off their mics, but make it clear that that option isn't permission to fade into the background.

  Have good audio. Make sure that those tuning in remotely have good audio. This means that they should be using headsets, and landline phones are better than the VOIP or computer audio, if there's an option. If there's a speakerphone in the conference room, and the remote contributors are on a speakerphone, you have a recipe for bad connections, garbled audio, and an audience that tunes out. Set expectations before the call, and hold people accountable for the quality of the audio.

Monitor the speakerphone. Don't allow the noise in the room to drown out important conversation and discussion. Appoint a monitor to keep the squawk box clear of noisy distractions and to bring the leader's attention to someone remote who's trying to contribute or ask a question.

Use chat proactively. Many meeting leaders try to limit chat because they find it distracting; but it's often a great way to get the best input from people. Some folks are shy and don't like to interrupt speakers to contribute by voice. Those for whom English is a second language (or third, or fourth) often find that it's easier to write out their thoughts than struggle with accents and bad audio. The team may be full of introverts or people who actually like to put a coherent thought together before opening their mouths. Allow people to contribute in a way that's both comfortable and effective.

- ◆ **Gather information.** You can gather information the same way you do in a traditional meeting. As I mentioned earlier, we gather a lot of information in the course of a meeting. Who has experience with that customer? How many people have used Basecamp in the past? Who thinks this suggestion is a recipe for disaster? Most tools have multiple ways of gathering information ranging from formal (polling and survey tools, emoticons, chat, or mark-up tools such as check marks or Xs) to a simple voice vote or show of hands.

Deliver Information in Multiple Ways

Project planning meetings contain a lot of information. Some is in the form of collected data, while some will come as stories told by experienced team members. The important thing to remember is that human beings absorb information in multiple ways. A good meeting provides more than just one form of communication. After all, if you're just showing spreadsheet after spreadsheet, you may as well email it out and save everyone the aggravation.

Here are some of the ways virtual meetings can help provide information:

- **Show as well as tell.** People are visual creatures. We want to see what you're talking about. To put it cynically, we also have the attention span of raccoons, and having something to look at that supports the topic under discussion will help keep us focused on that rather than on our email.

- **Use screen sharing to show spreadsheets or demonstrate software.** If you'll be showing a lot of information, though, consider uploading your content (slides, PDFs, etc.) so that you can quickly switch from one piece of information to another. Just as in a regular meeting, you can move from a PowerPoint presentation to a whiteboard to a handout and back, uploading the content to the software (available in just about every virtual meeting platform except the Citrix/GotoMeeting products).

- **Use whiteboards to maintain focus and communication.** People retain information when they see it and hear it. By using a whiteboard or a flip chart in a traditional meeting, you can get the best of both worlds. Most platforms have whiteboard features that serve the same purpose. You can capture input from discussions and brainstorming sessions, while leaving them up for visual reinforcement. You can also save the whiteboards from most web meeting tools. Many videoconferencing systems tie to smart whiteboards in the meeting room as well.

- **Upload content in advance to maximize the tools of the platform.** Presentations are efficient, and there's less dead time when you're changing speakers or content. A smoothly run meeting makes for a quicker, more-effective meeting and less frustration for everyone.

- **Use file transfer or attachments to share information without leaving the meeting.** Just as in a traditional meeting, you might have documents to hand out that you don't want people to see in advance. Most virtual meeting platforms have file transfer features that allow you to send people the file in question without resorting to using email (which might force them to leave the meeting to get it).

- **Answer questions and objections anyone might have as quickly as possible.** One of the most common and most self-sabotaging behaviors that facilitators exhibit in virtual meetings is to cram all the information in up front and ask people to hold their questions until the end. That's not how people process information. In a traditional meeting you'd say something and look at the audience and see confusion or resistance or understanding; then you could respond to the visual feedback you're getting. In a virtual meeting you're not getting the same visual cues, so you're not likely to see the confusion, resistance, or understanding and respond appropriately.

- **Allow full participation during presentations.** Encourage people to ask questions or get clarification before the presenter gets too far down the road. This means allowing people to unmute themselves, use the raise hand feature, or ask questions in chat.

   This may seem like a distraction for the speaker, but it doesn't have to be. Appoint a copilot whose job is to monitor the chat and watch people's faces on video to see who might have questions or who might have points to add to the discussion. That way the speaker can focus on content, and the copilot can gently interject when necessary.

- **Build Q&A into your presentation as you go, rather than at the end.** You've been in meetings where someone outlines a three-step process, then calls for questions. Inevitably the first question is, "Can you go back to step one?" You'll find that if people can question along the way, there will be better understanding, less frustration, and ultimately more effective time management for your meeting. The problem is that we have to plan for this interaction, and it's easy to get caught up in what you're doing and not take the time. Build pauses for questions and comments into your PowerPoint deck or program notes.

Collaborate to Create New Documents, Brainstorm, or Develop Processes

Virtual meeting tools can help draw out participation from remote attendees, focus the attention of the easily distracted, and help foster a sense of commitment to the task or outcome. Assuming that you use, them, of course. Here are some suggestions:

- **Get input early and often.** Using a whiteboard to have people make suggestions, identify common concerns, or create a list of questions, not only helps the leader make sure that people are getting what they need from the meeting, but it's also a very effective way to engage people early in the meeting. The longer people wait before contributing, the less likely they are to engage fully.

- **Use a whiteboard or a work-around.** As we mentioned earlier, the whiteboard feature is at least as useful as using a whiteboard or flip chart in a traditional meeting. (In some ways it's better – it never runs out of paper, the markers always have plenty of ink, and the good ones, such as Skype for Business, even have spellcheck!) If your platform doesn't have a whiteboard feature, have a copilot use a Word doc to capture information as the meeting goes along, and they can share their screen with the audience.

- **Make sure you hear from everyone.** There are a few features in most platforms that will help you do a better job of engaging participants. Some are obvious, some you may not have thought of as facilitation tools.

  - **The participant list should be visible.** Knowing who's on the call at all times is really helpful. Who haven't you heard from yet? Who do you know has knowledge worth sharing? The participant list is a huge advantage virtual meetings have over mere conference calls or video conferencing. You can also send private chat messages directly from the list.

  - **Set the rules often and show participants that you mean it.** Meeting behavior is often a result of conditioning, and often there are no consequences for non-participation. You should set expectations early – participants are expected to introduce themselves, ask questions when they have them, and contribute to the discussion. Periodically call on people, give them a chance to contribute, and allow them to do it in a way that's comfortable for them.

- **Use chat to give fair warning to those not participating.** Often I like to send a private chat message to someone who's been quiet so that I can make sure they're prepared before I call on them. That way I don't risk calling on someone who's gone to the bathroom or taken a phone call. That's just embarrassing for both parties.

- **Set meeting permissions for maximum collaboration before the meeting starts.** Most virtual meeting platforms allow you to control the amount of interaction in a meeting – who can chat with whom, who can present content, who can write on the whiteboard, and so on. Decide early on what you want people to do during the meeting and set those permissions before the meeting starts. That way you don't have to think too hard about it in the moment, and you send a subtle message that passive attendance isn't expected or appreciated.

- **If you have groups of people in different locations, assign room copilots.** When everyone's online, it's easy to use polling or other ways of allowing each person a vote. If everyone's in the same room, it's even easier. But when you have small groups gathered in conference rooms scattered all over the country, use a designated person from each group to count hands and help make sure that questions are answered and people are contributing.

Ensure Understanding and Buy-in

In a traditional meeting, you can look around the room and see heads nodding in agreement, bored looks of complacency, or eyes widened in panic. Those are important clues that tell you whether you can proceed with the meeting as planned, need to take a deeper dive into something, or can skip ahead. In a virtual meeting you're missing many of those signs that people understand and buy into what's being said. So you need to find a way to get that feedback and to let people know that it matters if they're on board or not. Virtual meeting platforms aren't as helpful with feedback as you might like, but here are a few best practices that you should use:

- **Use polling or surveys to capture important information.** Many of the platforms have polling tools that can ask questions that will give you important information. "On a scale of 1–5, how confident are you . . . ." or "Do you feel ready to move on?" Using these tools also allows you to see how many people are actively engaged, since they tell you the number of attendees who have or have not participated.

- **Don't ask non-specific questions.** You'll notice a huge difference in the number of responses and the quality of input if you replace non-specific questions such as "Any questions?" with more specific, queries. "What else might get in the way of success?" is a very different question from, "Anyone have anything else?" Again, get both oral and written input.

- **Use the whiteboard to brainstorm, then narrow down solutions.** Most whiteboard tools have annotations or stamps, such as check marks and Xs, that allow people to vote on options. By allowing participants to create lists of action items and then vote for their top solutions or priorities, you'll help build consensus. Traditional meeting techniques, such as using a five-point system for scoring options or the nominal group technique for problem solving (see Glossary), work exceptionally well in a virtual environment.

Leave People Feeling Energized and Positive about the Kickoff

This is more of a mind-set issue than a technical one. You only get one chance to make a first impression, to coin a cliché. If people feel like they've been on the Bataan death march, the project won't get off to a positive, energetic start. If, on the other hand, people believe that their time was well spent, that their initial questions were answered, that they'll be heard as the project continues, and that the leader (that's you) knows what they're doing . . . . Well, the less misery the better. Here are some tips for making a good first impression:

- **Record the meeting.** It's likely that your whole team won't make the meeting. Use the recording feature to ensure that stragglers, latecomers, and those who were putting out fires have the opportunity to get to know their teammates, hear the discussion, and hear the same information. Also, when people know they're being recorded (don't record them without fair warning) there's no room for "Oh, I didn't commit to that."

- **Set permissions so everyone can download everything they need.** Allow everyone to save the whiteboards, PowerPoint files, chat transcripts, and other information for themselves. It saves you (or some other poor soul) from having to transcribe and email everything out, and they can save the files where they'll be able to find them on their own.

- **Make sure that the team members know where to find information, and get them using it from day one.** Tools such as SharePoint, Workfront, Basecamp, and Slack are terrific, if people actually use them. Make these shared files part of the work process. Don't email people files. Instead send them the link to where those files can be found even when you're not around. Your kickoff meeting is supposed to set the tone for the work going forward. This includes not driving your project manager crazy with requests from team members for data that they should be able to find on their own.

- **Make a point of saying to the team members, out loud, how thankful you are for their participation and hard work.** And keep saying it until they believe you. With virtual meetings it's hard to stay focused and engaged. When people put the effort in, it should be acknowledged. That way there's a better than even shot that they'll stay engaged during the next meeting as well.

Facilitating good virtual meetings is a skill that needs to be developed. It requires being mindful of the dynamics before, during, and after the meeting that can make or break this critical first time together. In our work at the Remote Leadership Institute, we've learned two things that are important:

◆ **There's no way to avoid a learning curve.** You have to practice with these tools to use them effectively. If you don't practice you'll avoid using them, even when they can add great value.

◆ **It takes about half a dozen times using these tools for them to become muscle memory.** Once you've mastered them, you can focus on the really important tasks and your role as a successful project manager.

Some Hybrid Meeting Tips

If you have some team members attending remotely and some in person, here are some strategies for making sure they're all part of the action:

◆ Do it old school on the whiteboard and broadcast the whiteboard/flipchart to the remote attendees. There are multiple ways to do this, but if you're in a room with traditional video conferencing it's easiest. You can also go full-screen on WebEx to blow the picture up.

◆ Some platforms such as Skype for Business and Adobe Connect have whiteboards that create text boxes that can be dragged and dropped across the screen like sticky notes.

◆ Use a software tool such as Stormboard or RealTimeBoard and share the application. Both of these use virtual sticky notes for online brainstorming. I know that there are many other tools like them out there, but I'm not familiar with them, although online brainstorming is a hot topic in collaboration circles right now, so you should be able to find information about them online.

CHAPTER ELEVEN

Alternatives to Two-Day Meetings

I N THIS CHAPTER we'll discuss two options that you can choose from if the standard two-day project planning meeting doesn't work for you.

OPTION ONE
One-Day Conference Room Meeting with Functional Teams

Bringing together a large, multifunctional team requires not only a lot of upfront planning but also the meticulous scheduling of everyone's time. Sometimes this simply can't be arranged if team members' job functions won't allow them to take that much time away from their jobs.

One of us worked on a bank project whose goal was to rebrand the entire organization. They were going to come up with a new company name, a new website, business cards, signage – everything. And while they were a good, well-run bank, they had no real how to run a project of this magnitude. Project management, especially on this scale, was not their forte. Go-live dates had already been submitted to the board (and missed at least once.) We did discuss the idea of having a two-day planning meeting, but it wasn't possible to pull people from their normal workload for two days.

However, it was possible for teams to prepare as if we were going to hold such a meeting. Prior to getting together we met with the VP of finance, who was in charge of the project. We advised her that we needed each function to be able to provide us a list of activities that they needed to do and also to think about how those activities interrelated to other functions and when they needed to be done.

We then requested to have a conference room available for one day. As facilitators, we would stay in the room all day with different functions visiting us for an hour at a time (see chapter 10 on options for virtual attendance). In that room along with us were the VP of finance, who had much institutional knowledge, and an instructor who wanted to learn project management.

Since no one in the organization had any real project experience, we created a template using Microsoft Project that displayed a typical bank project. The purpose of this was to give the first group a tangible idea of what our output would look like. Essentially it was a dummy project so that the first team would know what output we were expecting. When the first group, mortgages, came in, we started to populate a blank project with their activities.

At first it was confusing. They'd never worked with a Gantt chart before, so that concept had to be explained. But in a short time they began to understand that we were simply trying to identify activities and understand how they would be connected. (Note that, in this method, we'd in effect skipped over the step of creating a WBS, which wasn't the best project management practice, but it saved significant time.) As we discussed these activities, someone would say, "But this affects the loan department in this way," and we'd note that on a flip chart. Or, "This new technique is somewhat risky," and we'd note that as well.

After an hour a second team entered the room. Instead of seeing a template of a *fake* banking project, they were now looking at a Gantt chart displaying their *real* project. The work that the first group had done helped make it easier for them to understand what we were attempting to do. They too noted activities either on the schedule or on a parking lot flip chart. Risks, dependencies, and assumptions were also noted.

As the day wore on, with other functional teams joining the room, this process made more and more sense to the VP and the instructor. The

VP at one point said, "I see where you're going with this." This was the *ah-ha moment* we'd hoped for. Our goal was to teach them to fish, as it were, so that they could replicate this process in the future.

By the end of a very long day, all functions had visited us and shared their story at least once. Some, excited by what they saw happening, would come back spontaneously with more input. But the good news is that we now had some semblance of a schedule, however rough. It was clear to everyone that we had made good progress but that we still needed to finalize the schedule.

For reasons of version control as well as familiarity with MS Project, it was agreed that we, the facilitators, would temporarily own the schedule and make any necessary updates to it. But instead of us routinely making the two-hour drive back to their facility, it was agreed that the VP and the instructor would do the in-person follow-up. By now they knew exactly which questions to ask and what information to chase down.

We then set up a few sessions to make regular updates to the schedule by means of a virtual connection. Only a few virtual sessions were needed, and in each instance, the instructor was the liaison to update us and we modified the schedule. After the call, we put the PDF in a shared online folder. (Again, for reasons of version control, we didn't initially send her the MS Project file.) She then used that updated schedule to gather more information from the various teams.

Now, strictly speaking, if they had had no one to do the follow-up, we would have gladly done it. But this situation worked out well – they were learning, and quickly, what steps were necessary to produce not only a schedule but a *viable* schedule that everyone could buy into with a high level of confidence.

And while this wasn't a training session per se, we did teach the fledgling project manager a few things of importance. For example, during schedule development it's typical for the critical path to be in flux. So, sometimes the website development was on the critical path, sometimes it wasn't. We taught them to be cognizant of these changes and to understand where there's float in the schedule and how to use it.

After a few of these back-and-forth sessions, our next in-person meeting a few weeks later was called by the CEO of the bank. He wanted to thank the teams for their hard work, make sure everyone understood the full nature of the project, and review the schedule with everyone. (We were fortunate in that the CEO had had some project experience, so he had a firm understanding of the Gantt chart.)

During the meeting we made some minor modifications to the schedule and some decisions about which items must be functional on the go-live date (website, ATMs) and which could wait (new outdoor signage.) The CEO advised us that he felt very confident in the proposed date and had already announced it to the board. There would be some nights and weekends involved, but they were determined to make that date.

The next meeting that we were involved in was the team's first real status meeting. The instructor had never run one before and wanted us to come in and help set an agenda for the session, determine which items were important and which were not important to discuss, and better understand how to keep the session from getting out of control.

The instructor took over the schedule (and the initiative) and drove the team to completion. We're happy to report that, minus a few of those items that were deemed non-essential, on the launch date, when customers logged into the old site, they were redirected to the new site and everything worked as planned.

The last in-person meeting we had with the team was a lessons learned session where we discussed what had gone well and what could have been done better. We'll discuss elsewhere in this book how to run such a session, but suffice it to say that the biggest lesson learned was to plan for these types of endeavors much earlier. And don't quote dates to management until you have a high level of confidence.

The credit belongs to the team for actually completing those activities that needed to be done in order to have bug-free software, correctly printed business cards, new signage, etc. But without the preparation and the successful facilitated meeting and follow up, the rebranding project probably wouldn't have gone well. And the team understood that.

The instructor wound up going to a three-day class on using Microsoft Project and invested in some other training. And while the bank has never again run a project of quite this size, they have successfully applied these techniques to other projects.

OPTION TWO
One-Day Meeting with Functional Managers

It's often not possible, or desirable, to interrupt team members' work. So another alternative to the one-day conference-room idea is to facilitate that same meeting, but this time with only the functional managers comprising the team.

The first step would be to advise the functional managers by conference call of the goal of the meeting. In this case the goal would be to develop a very rough, high-level schedule and to create an initial risk register.

During the call, ask the managers to think about the project not only from their team's perspective but also from the perspective of the larger goal. Let's say it's a pharmaceutical company and they're developing a drug. There may be regulatory issues that need to be considered, such as which countries they can sell it in, what clinical trials are required, etc.

Also during the call, display a Gantt chart that shows what the end goal is. Advise the managers that you would like them to go to their teams (or team leads) and get as much detailed information as they can about the activities that are needed to successfully deliver the overall project as well as key contributing milestones. They can collect this information in a spreadsheet. To the extent possible, they can try to determine how the activities are linked.

Schedule a face-to-face meeting as soon as possible after the conference call. Let each functional manager present, formally or informally, the project from their point of view. Have a couple of flip boards so you can capture ideas, risks, and issues in a free-form style.

Once the functional managers have spoken, bring up your scheduling tool and, starting with one of the functions, begin to populate the Gantt chart. Don't expect to get through this easily. The very act of adding activities to the schedule and trying to determine dependencies will bring up passionate discussions about who's doing a particular activity and when. Expect to hear that there aren't enough resources to do a particular thing. Capture that information.

As many as possible of the functional managers should be present and focused for the entire day. Set expectations. In the best-case scenario you'll be able to send each manager a PDF of the schedule for them or their leads to track down more information. Depending on the size of the project, it may be necessary to have a follow-up meeting with individual managers prior to going back to the team.

If a follow-up meeting is necessary, schedule it for as soon as possible after the first one, and make every attempt to schedule it while everyone is still in the room. Otherwise, as likely as not, you'll spend a lot of time chasing them down.

Once you get through meeting with the functional managers, where the project goes depends on how much they want you to be involved. If you're a full-time project manager, you should schedule separate sessions with either team leads or small, focused sub-teams to flesh out the schedule. At this point the work is no more than traditional project management – chasing down the activities, risks, issues, etc.

What you've accomplished by having these initial meetings with functional managers is to educate and enlighten them on what needs to be done in order to be successful on the project. You've also encouraged their buy in, which always increases the odds of success.

Once the schedule and risk register have been iterated to everyone's satisfaction, another functional manager meeting should be held just to make sure that everyone agrees with, and can sign off on, the baseline schedule.

These alternatives to the two-day meeting are meant to expedite the planning activities by sacrificing some of the things that ideally should be done, such as engaging in team-building, encouraging buy in, and creating a detailed work breakdown structure (clearly identifying the scope of the project) which will help you create a viable schedule. Should you choose one of these methods, be aware of the trade-offs you've made, and pay extra attention to validating the resulting scope of the project to be sure that you have captured 100 percent of the work that will generate a successful outcome.

CHAPTER TWELVE

Adding an External Customer Meeting

I N SOME CASES THE KICKOFF MEETING HAS TWO PARTS – one for an internal team, and then a "real" meeting in which the customer takes part. One of us oversaw dozens of such paired meetings for telecom deployments of new-technology products, on behalf of a firm that supplied telecom equipment and services. The internal portion was for the product teams, installation supervisors, test engineers, sales team members, and other workers. This was a critical meeting, but it had far too much detail for the customer. The expression "no need to see how the sausage gets made" applies here.

In our case, the sales team took the lead in ensuring that everyone at the internal kickoff meeting knew the rationale for the customer to launch the project and what they wanted to get out of it but also why the project was important to us as a telecom equipment supplier. This step, often missing at a project launch, is worth the investment of time.

That done, the next step was a shorter, sharper, well-orchestrated meeting for the customer, in which we, the well-oiled, well-prepared project team, could express not only what we were going to build for the customer but how (in milestone-chart detail, not Gantt chart detail) we would do it.

The customer meeting can include, or even be centered around, a meal – a relaxed setting in which the project team members from the supplier and their peers from the customer can get to know each other on a more personal level. If that option isn't available, be sure that you have a good way to introduce everyone and assure that roles are clear. This can be facilitated by a very good internal meeting, and the sales organization should have the accountability for knowing who does what, and which customer stakeholders are decision makers.

The agenda items for a customer meeting should focus on:

- Confirmation that "we heard you" in terms of requirements that need to be met.

- Assurance of the quality of the project team and the level of project management expertise available to them. One way to do this is to go around the room during introductions, asking how many years of project management experience each individual has accrued, and adding up this number. We have had many meetings in which we can state, after these introductions, that "there are three and a half centuries of project management experience in the room." That usually gets peoples' attention.

- Clarity between the supplier and the customer as to responsibilities. For example: how will the supplier be assured that they have access to the customer's sites as needed

- Establishment of inter-company communications, minimizing pairwise communications but at the same time maximizing the necessary pairing of individuals who need to share technical information.

- Assurance of the technical know-how available to the project team, and an expectation that the project team knows how to manage a project.

As long as these elements are covered, you can adapt a meeting agenda (in the appropriate order and length for each discussion item) as needed for your project.

CHAPTER THIRTEEN

Facilitating a Lessons Learned Meeting

IT SHOULD BE MANDATORY AT THE END OF EVERY PROJECT – and, if possible, at the end of every phase of a larger project – to hold a lessons learned meeting. And not only hold it, but make sure that it's documented and, unless it's highly sensitive, available to all future projects. We're talking about projects that you will manage (so you're the customer of these lessons learned) or projects that others will manage. Either way, that future project manager is going to benefit from the proper collection of lessons learned. Here's how to do it:

- ◆ **Be sure that you have an agenda.** People hate to come to meetings and not know what will be discussed or for how long.

- ◆ **Invite the right people.** Do whatever you can to schedule the meeting so that key stakeholders can attend. If some are available remotely or by Skype, fine. It's better that they attend that way than not at all. In the worst case, in their absence, you can collect their lessons and bring them to the meeting for two purposes: (1) so that the absent stakeholders know they're being heard, and (2) so that their lessons can trigger other ideas, memories, and lessons.

- ◆ **Meet as soon as possible.** Memory is a fleeting thing. Strike while the iron is hot and meet no later than two weeks after the close of the project.

- **Keep it short.** In addition to running our own sessions, we have solicited input from many practitioners. The great majority tell us that they can run a lessons learned session in one to two hours. People hate meetings, so keep it short.

- **Solicit input prior to the meeting.** Think of this as having students properly prepared for an important class discussion, or having read the book before attending a book club meeting. This can help you weed out what's important to discuss and look for common themes.

- **Provide multiple ways of attending.** Some people are just too busy. Can you set up a poll? Or have them email you information? That way their voices are heard and recorded. They feel like part of the process, and their thoughts aren't excluded.

- **Don't get sidetracked.** It's easy for meetings of any sort to get derailed. If, for example, there's a technical issue, some team members will be inclined to want to discuss and solve the problem in the meeting. Even worse, the meeting may be seen by some as a chance to blame people for things they may or may not have done (see "Set the tone" below). You need to remind them that they're not in a problem-solving, nor blame-assigning, nor even a credit-lavishing meeting. Have a parking lot flip chart for issues such as these that arise. They can go on your issue log to be dealt with in a separate session.

- **Set the tone.** You want to make it clear that the meeting is not a finger-pointing exercise. All the team members should care about is what didn't go well and what can they could do better, and what they did that was surprisingly good and should do again.

- **Keep good minutes.** Team members are going to make observations that are crucial. Keep track of them and make sure that you record and follow up on any action items. Tip: it may be a good idea to assign a couple of people to keep notes (which you can reconcile later).

- **If necessary, use a facilitator.** In most cases there's no reason that the meeting can't be run by the project manager. If, however, during the project, animosity developed between the project manager and various departments or stakeholders, then bring in a consultant or someone from the PMO to defuse the situation (or at least run the meeting). Having a facilitator also frees up the project manager to more thoughtfully contribute their *own* lessons learned.

- **Work the issue, not the person.** If it turns out that a lot of problems point back to one department or even one person, make sure to emphasize that this isn't a blame game. Any good functional manager will probably long since have recognized the problem. If no corrective action is taken post-meeting, meet with the functional manager and/or escalate to the sponsor. This works the other way as well. If project success all seems attributable to Bob, what was it about Bob that made a difference? We can't have Bob on every project, but we can find out what knowledge, skills, and attributes he brought to the project that can be duplicated on other projects.

- **Acknowledge your own imperfections.** Acknowledge that you could have, say, published the schedule in a timelier fashion. If others see that you're willing to be self-critical, they may be more forthcoming in their opinions.

- **Document and distribute.** We've met far too many people who, after running a meeting, put the documentation in a drawer, never to be seen again. Circulate it for comment, then put it in a centralized, hopefully easily-searchable repository for consideration by subsequent project teams. Each project has new challenges, but there's no need to reinvent the wheel.

    1. Write up some questions. You need to ask, at least, these three questions:

    2. What went well?

    3. What didn't go well?

    4. What might we do differently next time?

Make lessons learned meetings a habit. Otherwise you'll treat every project as brand-new and never be able to continuously improve.

CHAPTER FOURTEEN

Facilitating a Status Meeting

YOU MAY BE WONDERING why we would write a chapter on something so seemingly innocuous as running a regular status meeting. Well, one of us consulted to a company where an instructor was transitioning into becoming a project manager. While she had good instincts, she required our help in setting up and running her first meeting. So we realized that not everyone knows how to facilitate even simple meetings. And there are always new and best practices to learn.

The main reason to hold a regular status meeting is simple – you need to know exactly what's going on in your project at any given time, and your team needs to know the key elements. You need to have an up-to-date schedule, risk register, and issue list to review. If your sponsor or other stakeholder stops you in the hall, you should be able to say what the status of your project is.

You also need to be able to gauge the temperature of the team. How's the project going for them? What roadblocks are they encountering? Are they able to resolve them, or do you need to help them in some way, such as providing needed resources or expertise?

As we mentioned, the smart project manager uses the status meeting to review the risk register. Have either the impact or probability gone up or down? Was a risk response initiated? Is the response working? Did that cause any secondary risk or leave any residual risk? Can a risk be closed?

As to issues, you need to know what's happening now and what actions are being taken to resolve them and by when.

In short, you and your team need to come out of each status meeting with a high level of awareness of exactly where the project is now and what must be done next. Hopefully, if you've been tracking regularly, there will be no surprises.

Some Things to Take into Consideration

- **How often should you meet?** There's no right answer to this question. On a multi-year project status meetings could be held every two weeks. If the project is shorter than that, perhaps weekly. You want to have the right balance of meeting time versus work time.

- **Agenda? – Yes, yes, and yes.** Your kickoff planning meeting has an agenda – why should this meeting be any different? People want to know why they're there. Publish an agenda early and often. In fact, the best agendas have durations of time associated with them – how long will we discuss updating of tasks, how much time will we spend on the risk register? Be careful not to have your status meeting usurped by the crisis of the week. If you have an urgent situation that requires attention, schedule a separate, dedicated meeting for that.

- **Attendance matters.** You can't get status from people who aren't there. Make sure that project team members from all of the contributing functions are present or are represented. Take our case study: If the person responsible for installing the Tesla roof isn't going to be at the meeting, you still need to know that the roof is mechanically installed but the electrical testing won't take place until two weeks from now due to cloudy weather and/or the fact that Harry forgot where he keeps the voltmeter.

- **Manage the meeting.** You can't allow that person who always monopolizes meetings with war stories to monopolize your meeting with war stories. Or anecdotes. Or problem solving. If the meeting gets derailed and you don't get to your full agenda, your team members will be frustrated. They'll blame you, not that guy. And they'll be right. (See "Meeting Goblins," p. 28)

That said, sometimes there's a pressing technical problem that needs to be socialized. People will need to talk about it so they have some sense of progress. It's a judgment call on your part as to whether you allow this discussion into the meeting. The best thing you can do is to understand the problem and who the fixers are, and suggest that another session be scheduled just for that issue.

◆ **You need a timekeeper.** Someone must say, "Time to move to the next agenda item." You may think that you're being intrusive, but others will welcome this. If you don't get the meeting unstuck, it will be seen by people as intruding on their valuable time.

◆ **Meeting minutes matter.** You should publish meeting minutes, however brief, after every status meeting. The minutes should display any actions, with owners, resolution dates, and open issues. In a perfect world, the project manager can run the meeting and take minutes. If you can't do this, don't abdicate your leadership role. Ask someone else on your team to take notes and send them to you.

◆ **Determine your next steps.** Don't leave the room without determining who's doing what and when. If there's a follow-up meeting to be scheduled, strike while the iron is hot. Try to schedule it before everyone leaves the room while they have their calendars.

◆ **Review the schedule.** Update the schedule at every meeting or shortly after. You should be able to determine if there's been any slippage.

◆ **Review the risk register.** Even though the buck stops with you regarding risk management, you should delegate ownership of specific risks to appropriate team members. They'll be responsible for watching the risks on a weekly basis, reporting to you if the probability or impact go up or down or if a risk can be closed.

CHAPTER FIFTEEN

The Importance of Team Building

IN PROJECT MANAGEMENT THERE'S NOTHING MORE IMPORTANT, more sacred than the team. A team that works together tends to get more done, faster and better, than a team that doesn't. After all, a project manager's charge is to get work done through others – and most of those others are your core project team. But you can't expect to bring a group of people together, however well they may know each other, and have a team automatically form. The process takes care and feeding.

Psychologist Bruce Tuckman (1965) published a famous study where he identified what's now known as Tuckman's stages of group development – four stages that teams go through that are inevitable for their growth (he later added a fifth stage). Those stages are (see Exhibit 15.1):

◆ Forming
◆ Storming
◆ Norming
◆ Performing
◆ Adjourning (or Mourning)

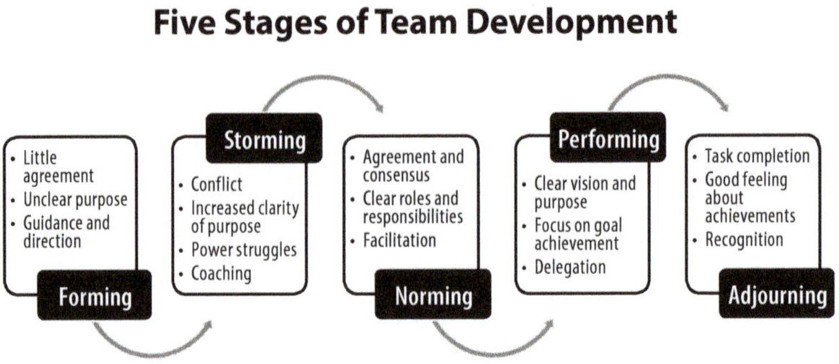

Five Stages of Team Development

Exhibit 15.1 Every team goes through five Ssages of team development. It's the job of the team leader to help see the team through these stages and bring them to a point where they're working as effectively as possible. Source: Okpalad, based on Tuckman and Jensen (1977).

Forming

In forming, the team meets and gets to know each other. Initially, team members are more focused on themselves and less on the team. The individuals look to the leader for direction and are still uncertain, not only of what the scope of their work is, but also their role and responsibility in it. People are also uncertain about how to behave, what to say, even whether jokes are appropriate. Needless to say, they're not yet a team; at this point what you have is a gathering of individuals.

At this early stage, the team is looking for leadership. You must establish clear goals and objectives and be cognizant of the fact that you'll soon be entering Storming. And be decisive – this is exactly what the team needs right now.

Storming

There's a good reason this stage is called Storming. In this stage, individuals are still getting to know each other, but they've now formed opinions about what each brings to the project. This stage is where conflicts and personality clashes start to arise. Tuckman says that some teams never grow out of this stage. In that case, while they may fulfill the objectives of the project, it will be a more painful process than if they had resolved their conflicts. Remember also that the conflict could be with the *project*.

In other words, a team member may not be fully on board with the overall project deliverable or one of its objectives. You'll need to have one-on-one conversations with such team members.

Tolerance and patience are important. The team leader is still very much in a directive status, not yet feeling comfortable delegating leadership. She may initially need more frequent meetings to find out how team members are working together and will likely be more heavily involved in conflict management. Storming can be destructive to the team and will lower motivation if it's allowed to get out of control – especially if the conflict becomes personal.

Some teams will never exit Storming. However, disagreements within the team can make members stronger, more versatile, and able to work more effectively as a team. Further, it's during the Storming stage that you'll likely find your more innovative ideas popping up, because competition and good arguments can stimulate creativity.

If a team never gets past this stage, it will be more difficult for it to deliver on time. The most important things at this point are to build trust as well as resolve conflict. Team-building (discussed below) can help to establish trust. As to conflict management, it's wisest to initially allow team members to work out their own conflicts. Step in to resolve them only if they can't.

Although a detailed treatment of conflict management is beyond the scope of this book, we have found that the Thomas-Kilmann Conflict Mode Instrument (Kilmann 2018) has significant value. This model yields five modes of dealing with conflict (see Exhibit 15.2). The five modes are:

- ◆ Competing
- ◆ Avoiding
- ◆ Accommodating
- ◆ Collaborating
- ◆ Compromising

According to TKI, each person has a default mode where they generally operate. But project managers need to be able to move easily between those modes for differing project situations.

That said, let's get back to team building.

Dealing with Conflict

Exhibit 15.2. Project managers need to be able to move easily between these modes of dealing with conflict for differing project situations, depending on whether it's best to be more assertive or more compromising. Based on the Thomas-Kilmann Conflict Mode Instrument.

Norming

In this stage the team starts to *cohere* as a team. If any members can't get along, they have by now left the team. The others are starting to work as a unit toward the project's objectives. The team members – and it's now a team rather than a group of individuals – are not only sharing responsibility but are acting more cooperatively with each other. It's in this stage where team members learn to trust one another. And while there is still very much a team lead, she's now able to allow the team to make its own decisions. If the leader is lost, or if there's any other disruption, it's possible for the team to fall back to a previous stage.

You must be careful not to slip back to an earlier stage for other reasons, such as unresolved conflict, hurt feelings, or lack of trust. If you need to do more team-building, do so. If a person needs to be removed from the team, do that.

Performing

In reality, this means *high-performing* teams. By this time, team members are motivated and knowledgeable. They're competent, autonomous, and able to handle the decision-making process without supervision. The team should now be automatically locked-in to the project's final deliverables and, without any direction, are keeping them in mind for all project decisions. Conflict may still arise, but team members will know best how to handle it, and the team leader is happy to let them do it. Group morale is high in this stage. Tuckman makes the argument that not all teams will arrive here, but it's incumbent upon your team to do so and for you to help them get there.

Adjourning

And so the team has been successful (or not . . .) and, alas, must disengage. This stage is sometimes called mourning – you've spent so much time building up a team relationship, and now you have to, in a sense, tear it down. Some team members may become emotional and want to stay together. You hear of this often in situations such as movie sets, where actors and crew are together for an intense month or two and develop a sense of family. For example, the entire cast of *A Fish Called Wanda* stayed together for a totally different film called *Fierce Creatures.*

As we mentioned, a key component of having an effective team is trust. Team members must trust that they can rely on each other to get the job done well. They must feel comfortable that team members will take individual responsibility and be accountable for their actions.

According to the *A Guide to the Project Management Body of Knowledge, (PMBOK® Guide), Sixth Edition,* high team performance can be achieved by employing these behaviors:

- Using open and effective communication
- Creating team-building opportunities
- Developing trust among team members

- ◆ Managing conflicts in a constructive manner
- ◆ Encouraging collaborative problem solving
- ◆ Encouraging collaborative decision making

Team-Building Methods

In our travels we've discovered that many project managers take an all-or-nothing approach to team-building. "We can't afford to send the team off to Outward Bound or some other offsite retreat," they'll say, "So we won't do *anything.*" Who says you have to give up on team-building because you can't take the team on an outing?

You can build the team in other ways. One of us recently joined a project where the team was 100 percent virtual. The product owner asked us to team up in pairs, interview each other, and create mind maps that would detail interesting facts about the other person. We then presented those on-screen in our meeting and got to know people on a personal level.

A caveat is that if you're planning to bring the team together to discuss your project and also do team-building, make sure that your efforts are effective. Case in point:

One of us contracted to a Boston-based company and became part of their distributed team. A one-day team-building session was planned. Other team members were brought in from around the country to join in. Prior to the meeting we were asked to provide the manager with a list of our accomplishments and play a game called "two truths and a lie." In that game one writes down two things that are true about oneself and makes something up.

At the meeting we all gathered around a table in a conference room. (There were about twenty-five people.) There was a large screen in the room and instead of us talking about and sharing our accomplishments, they were put up on the screen that pretty much no one read. So this exercise ended up having no purpose or meaning. Strike one.

Then we went around the table to introduce ourselves, but instead of getting a few minutes to tell something personal, all we could say was "Joe Smith, Dallas." So a second opportunity was squandered. When we finally teamed up to play "two truths and a lie," it felt hollow since it was impossible for us to guess anything about team members about whom we knew nothing. We weren't even paired up well.

Then we all went to a company facility where we looked at the history of the company, which was detailed in timelines on the wall. This afforded us no opportunity to interact. We then went to dinner, which provided us with the only real interaction we had had all day. But it was too little, too late. The general consensus was that while it was nice to get together, the team wasn't functioning as a team after this exercise any more than it had been prior to the meeting.

This lack of team building happened because there was very little *real* interaction. In order for team members to get to know each other, they need to perform exercises where they work toward a common goal. One popular exercise is the use escape rooms, where teams work together to find clues to escape a locked room.

If you'd like to accelerate the team member's getting to know each other with a quick and easy-to-implement exercise, we suggest Human Bingo. The use of this game will depend on the culture of your organization, but we've used it at conservative banks and energy firms with success. The steps are easy:

- ◆ Create bingo cards (5 × 5 square grid), and make sufficient copies for everyone.

- ◆ Customize the card to stimulate conversation by filling in the boxes with humorous and/or mildly controversial (or at least interesting) traits or characteristics. (See Exhibit 15.3)

- ◆ Give each attendee a card and a pen or pencil.

- ◆ Explain the rules:

  - • Each person is to go around the room, introduce themselves (name only) and either offer up a square or seek one from another player. When people pair up like this, the intent is that they each give the other one square.

  - • A square is attained by having the other individual write their name or initials on a square that accurately describes them – for example, "I am left-handed." Then the roles are reversed – each person walks away from the transaction with one, and only one, square signed by the other person. Each transaction should only last a few minutes.

135

B	I	N	G	O
I drive a hybrid or electric vehicle	I am afraid of heights	I wear contacts	I have been to Disneyworld or Disneyland	People tell me I am a good cook
I have a pet at home	I enjoy following politics in the news	I like to golf	I am good at technical things	I am the oldest child
I have gone skydiving	I have a "Summer" birthday (June–Aug)	Free Square	I play an instrument (not necessarily a virtuoso!)	I am the youngest child
I speak a language other than English	I've attended a professional soccer match	I was born in the same month as you	I can name at least one song from the musical "West Side Story"	I can juggle
I am left-handed	I am a member of PMI	I have a nickname	I have taken a cruise	I went to college outside (state or region)

Exhibit 15.3. Human Bingo is a great icebreaker. Customize a bingo card to help team members get to know one another quickly.

- ◆ Players continue to circulate, seeking a row (or rows) of signed squares (bingo!), or, depending on the amount of time, as many signed squares as they can get.
- ◆ Call time and end the exercise. For a group of twenty people, typically you can call time after twenty to twenty-five minutes.

- Declare the winner. Do a readout at the end by asking who made a bingo (horizontal, vertical, diagonal). Several people will usually have at least one bingo. If no one has a bingo you can ask, "Who has more than ten squares signed?" and ask people to leave their hands up as you ask, "More than eleven?" "More than twelve?" etc. The last person with their hand up is the winner. You can decide whether to have a token prize for the top performers.

This exercise usually provides not only a chance for team members to meet each other but also tends to bring a lot of positive energy to the meeting.

In addition to the Human Bingo exercise, your team-building budget might be able to cover fun activities such as bowling or some other sporting event. Even if the team isn't working together toward a common goal, it's in these informal situations where the pictures of the kids come out or people talk about their pets – and they become a lot more open to relationship-building.

And lastly, working together in the facilitated meeting that we discussed earlier in the book is a great way to build a team. Yes, there will be arguments, clashes, and conflicts of opinion during the session. But these are, or should be, healthy discussions, not negative interactions. It's the job of the facilitator and sponsor to keep it that way.

CHAPTER SIXTEEN

Facilitating Meetings in a Multicultural Environment

L ET'S START WITH A DEFINITION OF *CULTURE* from an expert we trust – Geert Hofstede. Hofstede, dubbed a guru and "the man who put corporate culture – literally – on the map," by *The Economist*, taught at the well-respected business school INSEAD, near Paris, and in Hong Kong. He also taught for long spells in his home country of The Netherlands, at Maastricht University and the University of Tilburg.

Early in his career Hofstede worked for IBM, where he carried out the research on which his career and reputation subsequently rested. What has become known as the Hofstede Cultural Orientation Model is based on his study between, 1967 and 1973, of IBM employees in forty different countries. He continues to pursue and publish up-to-date corporate culture studies, and he's often cited as the central reference for all things related to cultural differences (see geerthofstede.com).

According to Hofstede Insights (2018a):

Culture is defined as the *collective mental programming* of the human mind which distinguishes one group of people from another. This programming influences patterns of thinking which are reflected in the meaning people attach to various aspects of life and which become crystallized in the institutions of a society.

Next, it's important for us to gain an appreciation of two different aspects of culture, organizational and national (country) culture. Below we draw from Hofstede's research by picking and choosing some of the dimensions from both organizational and national culture.

Organizational Culture

Organizational culture is defined as "the way in which members of an organization relate to each other, their work and the outside world in comparison to other organizations. It can either enable or hinder an organization's strategy." (Hofstede Insights 2018b)

We have selected the dimensions of culture that most impact the success of your project planning meetings, and apply those dimensions to your meetings.

Means-oriented versus Goal-oriented

This dimension is closely connected to the effectiveness of the organization.

♦ In a means-oriented culture it's all about the *how*.

♦ In a goal-oriented culture employees are primarily out to achieve specific goals or results; however they are achieved – they are all about the *what*.

For project meetings, this aspect of organizational culture will be significant. In *means-oriented* cultures, you're likely to have strong buy-in for meetings – they recognize the fact that meetings are a means to an end. However, in goal-oriented cultures you'll likely have trouble even getting people *to* meetings, and you'll probably struggle to keep their attention.

♦ Here's a tip: Read them our section below on what it costs to *not* have meetings. This focus on results will appeal to their sense of accomplishment – it will tie the end to the means.

Easygoing Work Discipline versus Strict Work Discipline

♦ An easygoing work discipline culture is comfortable with lots of improvisation and surprises.

♦ A strict work discipline culture is the opposite – people are no-nonsense, punctual, and serious.

The connection is straightforward. In an easygoing culture it's going to be difficult to get people to meetings on time – or perhaps even to get them to take assigned action items seriously. The opposite is true of a strict work discipline culture. However, it's not that black and white. People from an easygoing work discipline, when they finally show up, will likely do well in an open brainstorming session, while their strict work discipline cousins pine for a more structured activity.

As a project manager you should be aware of this dimension of culture. You may need to shift your style from time to time to accommodate both. For example: For a WBS session, start on time, and explain to people how you expect this strict discipline style to work, but make sure that when you develop the WBS you allow and encourage creative, off-the-wall suggestions for WBS content. Indicate that the end-time of the meeting is uncertain because you want to allow it to fully play out.

Local versus Professional

This dimension is about how employees identify themselves. In a so-called local organization, employees tend to identify with the boss and/or the unit in which they work. "I'm in the XYZ Product Development Group," they're likely to say. Conversely, in a professional organization, an employee instead identifies with their profession. "I'm a senior programmer," they're likely to say. As a project meeting facilitator, this will be important because part of your job is to make sure your project team really clicks as a team, which means that you need to watch out not only for cliques – small groups that may sub-optimize the work you need to get done as one larger project team – but how they tend to form.

Open System versus Closed System

- In an open culture newcomers are readily welcomed, and the working belief is that almost anyone could join the organization.

- In a closed-system organization, the belief is that one has to be special, or be initiated, to join the organization.

Clearly, if you need to bring people together for project team meetings, you'll have much more trouble getting people past the Storming stage in a closed system. Refer to chapter 15 for advice on how to do that.

National Culture

National culture, like organizational culture, is made up of dimensions – this time *cultural dimensions*, which "represent independent preferences for one state of affairs over another that distinguish countries (rather than individuals) from each other." (Hofstede Insights 2018c)

Here we present the Cultural Dimensions of National Culture that most greatly affect project meetings. Again, we tie these dimensions directly to their effect on your meetings – how they may help or hinder them.

Power Distance Index (PDI)

- When the PDI is high, employees expect that everybody has their place (their rank), and higher rank automatically demands respect and has authority. Lower rank – well, they don't demand *anything*. They do what the higher-ranked person tells them to do.

- In societies with low PDI, people believe that power and authority should be equally distributed. As the leader of the meeting you may see a high PDI as an advantage ("All hail the Project Manager, Great Leader Of This Meeting!"), but it can be a detriment. With high PDI (Malaysia, Guatemala, Panama, Philippines, Mexico, Venezuela, China), those who perceive their power to be low won't interrupt or contribute, even when what they have to say may be critical.

As facilitator, you need to be aware of this dimension and the fact that it may prevail in certain national cultures – and knowing this, poll the audience and invite participation frequently. In low PDI cultures (Austria, Israel, Denmark) you won't have this problem, but you may have the other extreme – interruptions and disregard for authority. You may have to remind this audience that *you* own the meeting and assert control.

Individualism versus Collectivism (IDV)

- Individualism (high IDV) means that employees prefer a loosely-knit social framework in which individuals are expected to take care of and distinguish themselves.

- Collectivism (low IDV) is a preference for a group in which individuals can expect their relatives or members of a particular association to look after them in exchange for unquestioning loyalty.

For countries with high IDV (the United States, Australia, the United Kingdom, the Netherlands), people will likely be a little less shy and more willing to be creative and/or take a stance on an issue. In the extreme, they may even showboat and be less likely to be team players.

On the other hand, you may have to tease out contributions from low IDV countries such as many Central American countries, Pakistan, and Indonesia.

These same countries, however, are also more focused on team formation and team goals, but it's a mixed blessing: the team may form more quickly but may be less innovative and more risk averse. This is a good segue to the next dimension – uncertainty avoidance.

Uncertainty Avoidance Index (UAI)

UAI defines how a group feels with respect to uncertainty and ambiguity.

Think of a high UAI as being very risk averse, and a low UAI as being risk seeking. Getting buy-in on a project – which is by definition unique and therefore prone to uncertainty – will be harder with high-UAI countries such as Greece, Portugal, and Guatemala, and easier with low UAI countries, such as Singapore, Jamaica, and Denmark. Change management in general will be easier in the low-UAI countries, because changes are often perceived as big buckets of uncertainty, which low-UAI countries can tolerate, even enjoy.

You can go to www.hofstede-insights.com/product/compare-countries/ to compare countries along these dimensions. In Exhibit 16.1 you can see the striking difference between the United States and China in IDV and PDI, and even more so between Greece and China in UAI.

Culture Dimensions and Project Planning Meetings

The general guidelines above will help you to understand cultural differences. But we'd like to further illustrate with our own experiences.

The Thundering Table

One of us, attending his first meeting outside the United States, was tired after his first real international travel, and he finished his presentation

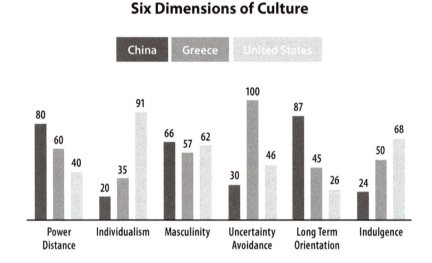

Six Dimensions of Culture

Exhibit 16.1. These six demensions of national culture are most likely to affect project meetings. You should account for cultural differences when structuring meetings. Here we compare the United States, China, and Greece. Based on the Hofsede Cultural Orientation Model (Visit hofstede-insights.com for a tool to compare other countries.)

somewhat bleary-eyed and waited for a reaction. He didn't have to wait long. He heard what sounded like a combination of thunder and amplified popping popcorn. The attendees were loudly pounding on the heavy wooden boardroom table. What had he done wrong to deserve this horrendous noise? Nothing, it turns out. This is how a German audience expresses its appreciation for a good technical or academic presentation, a tradition that apparently started in German universities.

Dutch Directness Dares to Deliver Delightful Doom

This actually is a good thing for risk identification during project planning meetings. One of us noted this sizeable cultural difference between the Dutch and the Americans while attending a risk planning meeting for a telecom network deployment. The Dutch attendees seemed to take great pleasure in identifying the threats – every single possible thing that could go wrong. To an American ear it sounded like *negativity*. It sounded like the annual meeting of the Pessimists Club. After hearing all of

144

these threats, he almost wanted to drop the project or, more accurately, run home, screaming in fear. However, the exercise shifted to the opportunities (the things that could go horribly *right*), and the Dutch were equally adept at identifying these. When all was said and done, even with the long list of threats on the flipchart, in bright red ink, staring at the attendees, they couldn't wait to get to a local pub and celebrate the start of the project. So much for the Pessimists Club!

What the Dutch colleagues realized was that they had permission to act as full-fledged pessimists during the risk identification process, without fear of being called nay-sayers. They also demonstrated that it's possible, and advantageous, to shift attitudes, taking on the pessimist's viewpoint to identify what may go wrong, without losing optimism for the project. Remember – unidentified threats have zero chance of having any sort of planned risk response. (Nazlieva 2018)

The Silent Treatment

One of us, after a fairly long and somewhat emotional presentation about sustainability in project management to a large Malaysian audience, was surprised at the near-silence at the end of his presentation. Had he failed to convey the idea? Had he somehow insulted his audience? Why wasn't anyone asking any questions? It turns out that in the Malaysian culture the audience needs to be prompted and encouraged to respond. Luckily, the conference organizers were aware of this and had arranged for audiovisual assistants with microphones to wander through the audience and indicate that it was appropriate to ask questions. This turned the tide, and a dozen good-quality, well-thought-out questions were asked with increasing enthusiasm. This is reminiscent of the behavior of some Asian audiences at rock concerts, at which they'll sit quietly during the performance and then raucously applaud and celebrate at the conclusion.

Give or Take a Couple of Students

One of us taught a project management course at a university in the Liaoning province of China. This was to be a two-weekend class, taught on Friday night and all day on Saturday and Sunday. On arrival at the airport on Thursday, an assistant dean picked him up in a university van to take him to the hotel and brief him on the final course logistics. "There's some major construction at the building in which you'll be teaching," she said. "In fact, there's a three-meter-deep trench dug all the way around the building, with no fences, signs, or lighting. You're teaching on Friday night; it will be very dark. Do you want to hold the class? We may lose a student or two." This was said without humor. It was a serious question. Aghast, he said, "No! We'll extend the Saturday and Sunday classes and teach through lunch." He remembered that the culture in China is much less risk-averse than in the United States, where that statement about losing a student or two would have made a great joke. This shows the value of understanding cultural differences.

Bowling for Business

One of us took an extensive course in Japanese language and culture. In the course, the instructor stressed the importance of your business card and the ceremonial nature of your presentation of the business card – you're handing your colleague your essence or face (as in saving face), so you must do it in a specific way. There's even a name for it – *meishi koukan* (名刺交換). Some of the students from the course visited Japan, and their first meeting was in a large, elongated room with a highly-polished mahogany table. The American attendees entered on one side, and their Japanese colleagues on the other. Seeing the long table, one of the Americans, despite all the coaching he'd received, simply couldn't resist the temptation and flung his card, bowling style, along the table. It was thrown skillfully, and skimmed easily almost the full length of the room. My instructor, who was also attending, nearly fainted. She said it was as if the person had hurled *himself*, like a rather indelicate human bowling ball, on the table and skittered toward his Japanese hosts. There was no laughing – this was a cultural faux pas for sure, and the colleague got a strong reprimand from our instructor, and she walked away with a very good story.

(See this video for further information on *meishi koukan*: https://blog.gaijinpot.com/exchanging-business-cards-japan/)

195 Countries Separated by a Common Language

One of us ran an IT project wherein his job was to oversee the deployment of software and hardware for an investment bank in New York City.

He had to communicate regularly with different parts of the country and with a few stakeholders in the United Kingdom. He was just starting to develop a relationship with a U.K. business person, and one day, during a phone call, they decided that a particular activity either was no longer needed or could be dismissed. He said, "Well then, let's just blow it off." ("Blow it off" is American slang for "let's avoid it" or "let's just not do it since it's not important.")

"Do *what*?" the Brit said. Realizing that he'd used an American expression, he tried to explain what it meant. Once the Brit understood its meaning, he calmed down a little. But his subsequent words still resonate – "Never use that expression again," he said. Clearly he found it somewhat offensive and highly colloquial. So, lesson learned. This works both ways.

The other one of us was debriefing after a project meeting, and his colleague in the United Kingdom said, "Well, Kathrine was quite stroppy in the meeting, wasn't she?" "Stroppy?" he said. "What does that mean?" "Oh, you don't know? That means easily angered . . . irritable . . . that sort of thing." Even though he's an American of rather advanced age with decades of international work experience, he had never once heard that word used.

These are examples of people from two *English-speaking* countries. We could give examples of the same issues between people from the six New England states, to say nothing of language differences between those from Maine and Texas. You can imagine that for people with English as a second (or even third) language, the chance for such expressions to confound communications is orders of magnitude higher. Pay attention to your use of colloquialisms. Take an extra moment to make sure that you're using language that will easily cross borders without making your attendees stroppy.

CHAPTER SEVENTEEN

Agile Project Planning

T HE AGILE ALLIANCE DEFINES *AGILE* as "the ability to create and respond to change in order to succeed in an uncertain and turbulent environment."[1] A driver behind agile is the difficulty of accurately understanding exactly what the customer requirements are at the outset of a project. To reduce threats while simultaneously increasing quality and the likelihood that the customer or stakeholders will accept a product or solution, agile incorporates various opportunities to validate and ensure that the solution will work.

In this brief chapter, we'll first provide a high-level overview of agile and how Scrum (a popular agile method) fits into the agile approach. We'll then talk about how agile is utilized in planning and scheduling and, finally, how it can be used at scale, similar to the emphasis on traditional project meetings demonstrated in this book.

The Tenets of the Agile Manifesto

In 2001, there was a mini-summit of seventeen development practitioners to discuss their ideas for better approaches to developing software. Instead of creating the next set of standardized processes and procedures, they approached software delivery from a values and principles perspective. The output was the Agile Manifesto, which states:

We are uncovering better ways of developing software by doing it and helping others do it. Through this work we have come to value:

- **Individuals and interactions** over processes and tools
- **Working software** over comprehensive documentation
- **Customer collaboration** over contract negotiation
- **Responding to change** over following a plan

That is, while there is value in the items on the right, we value the items on the left more.

While the original manifesto centered around software development, there has been much debate in the agile community regarding the possibility of expanding these concepts beyond software, and how to do it. Some teams these days are using agile for sales and even for recruiting.

Several important factors to note with the manifesto as it relates to scheduling, and in effect on meetings, include:

- Nowhere in the manifesto does it say *no documentation is required.* There's a certain level of documentation that does have value. You need to determine for your organization and industry (especially if you're in a regulated environment) the minimum level of documentation needed. If the documentation isn't used or consumed by another group, or a document is used in place of a conversation, then chances are this document has little to no value and should be considered for obsoleting.

- Agile is rooted in the ability to respond to change. But that doesn't mean there is *never any planning.* There's a common saying in agile: "You should plan to re-plan, and then re-plan, and then . . ."

Planning in agile is done continuously and in smaller chunks of time – a duration that enables enough working product to be created so that reasonable feedback can be obtained. Based on that feedback, re-planning happens. So instead of planning an entire project up front in detail, there's an emphasis on the act of planning (and the collaboration that ensues due to planning) versus having a firm plan that doesn't change, or is under strict change control.

What is Scrum?

There are multiple flavors of agile. Scrum is one of many approaches to agile.

The Scrum Guide (Schwaber and Sullivan 2017) says that Scrum is "a framework within which people can address complex adaptive problems, while productively and creatively delivering products of the highest possible value."[3] Strictly speaking, it's not a prescriptive methodology but, as stated, a framework. Scrum is based on empirical process control, that is, observations and evidence such as a detective might gather. It has three pillars – inspection, adaptation, and transparency.

Inspection means that the team(s) will produce increments of working product that the stakeholders will then interact with; stakeholders will give their opinions on the validity of the working product. *Adaption* means that the product owners will take the feedback and make adjustments as needed. *Transparency* means that communications will be open and visible to all; there is no hidden work or hidden opinions.

The components of Scrum include:

- Three roles: product owner, scrum master, and the team
- Five events or ceremonies: sprint planning, daily scrum, sprint review, sprint retrospective, product backlog refinement
- Three artifacts: product backlog, sprint backlog, and working product increment

Scrum teams are self-organizing and cross-functional. *Self-organizing* means that the team decides how to direct its own work rather than be directed by those outside the team. *Cross-functional* means that the team is composed of the various members needed to do the work of the project, or sprint, rather than having those teams exist in silos.

Common Scrum Terms Regarding Requirements?

Instead of collecting detailed requirements upfront, Scrum uses placeholders for requirements called product backlog items (PBIs), which are discussed and progressively refined throughout the project. The most common PBI is the user story.

- **User story.** A small piece of functionality that can be developed and tested, and which is potentially shippable in one sprint

◆ **Epic.** Requires significant effort and is composed of multiple stories

◆ **Theme.** A group of related stories

Using Scrum in Planning and Scheduling Your Project

In traditional plan-driven projects, the assumption is that you (or the customer) know what you want and are fully able to articulate your requirements. Yes, you can make changes but, by design, requests for modifications must go through change control, and, if approved, they're then put into production.

By contrast, in Scrum, the assumption is that the requirements are not fully understood at the beginning of the project. Instead, you'll learn more about the project as you proceed, and you are only expected to deliver incremental chunks of functionality in an iterative fashion. Change is the hallmark of Scrum, so, at least in theory, requirements (product backlog) can be reprioritized before every sprint begins.

In a Scrum environment, the stakeholders get to *see* working product with every iteration, and they can request course corrections along the way. The idea is that, when you're drafting requirements on paper, it's hard to truly articulate and understand what stakeholders really want. By frequently interacting with working product increments along the way, stakeholders get greater understanding and clarity of what it is they actually need.

If a Scrum team is using two-week sprints, in a six-month time frame, the stakeholders are able to interact with working product increments up to twelve times. By comparison, in a traditional project approach the stakeholders may only get to see the product one time, at the end of the six-month time period, which is risky.

Each sprint begins with planning – what are we going to accomplish in this sprint? What is our sprint goal? This planning will include the product owner, scrum master, and team. Once the team agrees on what work needs to be done and estimates the work, the work beings.

Each day the team meets in a fifteen-minute "standup," or scrum. Three questions are asked:

◆ What did I do yesterday?

◆ What will I do today?

◆ Are there any impediments in my way?

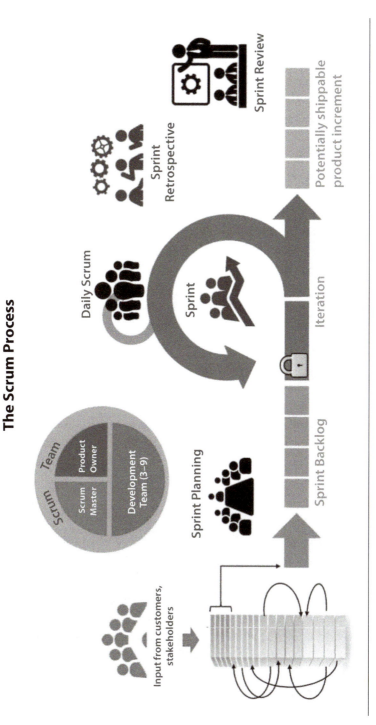

Exhibit 17.1. The Scrum process: Various Scrum events provide opportunities for inspection and adaptation. Courtesy of Heidi Araya, Agilist Extraordinaire.

The scrum master facilitates these sessions, but, unlike with traditional command-and-control project management, she doesn't tell team members what to do or even how to do it. That's up to the team. The scrum master's job is to facilitate and enable. He or she keeps the Scrum principles first and foremost and removes impediments (we need a room; we can't get software; there's too much interference from upper management.)

The sprint ends with a sprint review (a product demonstration where feedback on the product is obtained) and a sprint retrospective (a lessons learned session where continuous improvement ideas are identified and selected to be worked on in the next sprint(s)). Sprint reviews typically run four hours for a one-month sprint and include a discussion of the business context and update of the product backlog.

As the next sprint begins, the team chooses another chunk of the product backlog and begins working again. The team measures its velocity, which is the amount of work a team can accomplish in each sprint. They use this information as a projection for release planning. (See Exhibit 17.2)

Scrum Benefits

A major benefit in using Scrum is increased customer satisfaction due to greater customer involvement and engagement. In addition to producing high-performing teams, your products will be more aligned with the business's strategic objectives and provide exactly the functionality the business seeks.

Agile and Large Project Planning

The Agile Manifesto and framework do a very good job in describing life on a project for a single team. But as we've seen in our discussion on project planning, often there are multiple cross-functional teams involved in a project. For this, the Scaled Agile Framework (SAFe) was developed.

SAFe promotes alignment, collaboration, and delivery across *large numbers of agile teams*. It was developed, by and for practitioners, by leveraging three primary bodies of knowledge: agile software development, lean product development, and systems thinking.

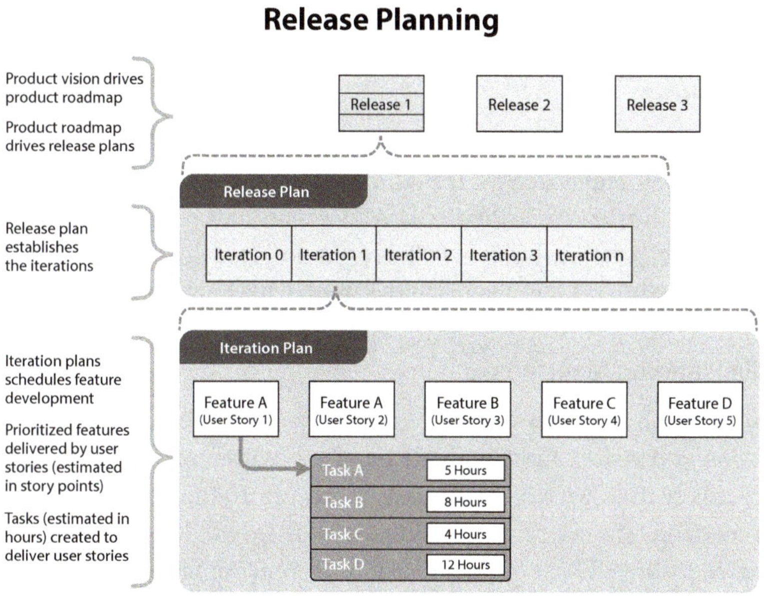

Release Planning

Exhibit 17.2. As a sprint begins, the team chooses a chunk of the product backlog and begins working. The team measures its velocity, which is the amount of work a team can accomplish in each sprint. They use this information as a projection for release planning. Copyright © Project Management Institute. Used with permission.

How Does SAFe Differ from Non-Scaled Agile?

SAFe introduces a concept called the agile release train (ART). This is defined as "a long-lived team of agile teams, which, along with other stakeholders, develops and delivers solutions incrementally, using a series of fixed-length iterations within a program increment (PI) timebox. The ART aligns teams to a common business and technology mission." (Scaled Agile 2018)

Program Increments

A PI is a timebox during which an ART delivers incremental value in the form of working, tested software and systems. PIs are typically eight to twelve weeks long.

The most common pattern for a PI is four development iterations, followed by one innovation and planning (IP) iteration. It's a fixed timebox for building and validating a full system increment, demonstrating value, and getting fast feedback.

New Roles

There is a new role called the release train engineer (RTE). The RTE is a servant leader and coach for the ART or team of teams. The RTE's major responsibilities are to facilitate the ART events and processes and assist the teams in delivering value. RTEs communicate with stakeholders, escalate impediments, help manage risk, and drive improvement.

SAFe Planning Meetings

PI planning is a face-to-face event that aligns all the teams with a shared mission and vision. Distributed teams may use remote communication methods such as we have discussed in chapter 10 in order to be part of the meeting. The planning meeting is typically two days long and is facilitated by the RTE, a coach of coaches who encourages cooperation. As in a large, more traditional, waterfall planning session, business context and vision are presented, followed by team planning breakouts. Essentially each team is a scrum team with its own scrum master and product owner. The planning meeting occurs during the IP iteration.

PI Planning Deliverables

There are two SMART (specific, measurable, achievable, relevant, timebound) objectives for each team aligned with business value, and a *program board*, which shows delivery dates, milestones, and dependencies among teams. Some will recognize the latter as a swimlane visual.

Meeting Activities

This meeting is very similar in some respects to a waterfall planning meeting. The business owner (sponsor) talks about how current customer business needs are being met. Product management talks about the product vision and milestones.

The RTE presents the planning process and expected outcomes of the meeting. Teams estimate their velocity for each iteration and identify backlog items. They begin working on their team PI objectives. Features get added to the program board.

Teams present their plans, which get critiqued by other teams and management. The goal is to find scope issues, risks, or dependencies. The RTE keeps everyone on track and facilitates discussion. It's not his or her job to direct proceedings.

On the second day, any results and changes from the previous day are discussed. Teams continue planning, incorporating necessary adjustments. Objectives are finalized, and the business owners assign business value.

During the final plan review, all teams present plans to the group. Risks and impediments are identified. No attempt is made to remove impediments in this time frame, but mitigation plans are made for any program-level risks.

Management Acceptance of Commitments

One method agilists use to gauge acceptance of a commitment is to execute the simple concept called *fist of five*, which is just holding up anywhere from one to five fingers to vote on something. Each team conducts a fist-of-five vote. If the average is three fingers or above, then management should accept the commitment. If it's less than three, the team reworks the plan.

Any items that don't have a vote of confidence might add to the list of risks or require re-planning. Teams are given the opportunity to rework their plans until there's a high level of confidence.

Lastly, as in Scrum, the RTE leads a retrospective for the PI planning event to record what went well and what didn't.

On leaving the PI planning event, teams and product owners have not only a good sense of the roadmap but also a backlog for the upcoming PI. The RTE maintains a list of the risks.

So you can see that the world of agile is different – it has different working assumptions, different terminology, different ways of working. Still, many of the overall tips and guidance in this book will apply to project meetings of either an agile or waterfall nature.

If you're seeking more information on how exactly to perform Scrum, you should certainly check out the Agile Manifesto along with its principles and the separate *Scrum Guide*.

- ◆ Agile 101, The Agile Alliance (www.agilealliance.org/agile101/)

- ◆ The Agile Manifesto (www.agilemanifesto.org)

- Scrum Alliance (www.scrumalliance.org)
- Scaled Agile Framework (www.scaledagileframework.com)
- *Scrum Guide* (www.scrum.org/resources/scrum-guide)

CHAPTER EIGHTEEN

The Costs of *Not* Holding a Project Planning Meeting

IN PROJECT RISK MANAGEMENT, one of the ways to respond to a threat is to Avoid, which the Project Management Institute (2017) defines as "when the project team acts to eliminate the threat or protect the project from its impact." We must realize that avoiding the threat also *avoids any of the benefit* from the eliminated activity or scope. For example, if you wanted to put the very latest, high-efficiency solar panels on our LEED house, but you're afraid of the new technology, we could avoid that threat by reverting to a prior-generation panel. We now have a well-known technology and have avoided the threat of the newer technology, but, alas, *we have also sacrificed the benefit that the new, more-efficient panels would have granted us.*

We could say that the philosophy to *not* run a meeting is a similar avoidance of threat – in this case, the threat of an additional project cost. In this chapter, we'd like you to consider the fact that you're also sacrificing some significant benefit when you decide to skip the meeting.

The problem is that many of the benefits of having a meeting are *intangible.* However, this doesn't mean they're non-zero – they're just hard to measure.

In an excellent book on how to measure, Douglas Hubbard (2014) says, "Some of the most important strategic proposals were being overlooked in favor of minor cost-saving ideas simply because everyone knew how to measure some things and didn't know how to measure others . . . Like many hard problems in business or life in general, seemingly impossible measurements start with asking the right questions." So we ask: What does it cost if you *skip* that (perhaps relatively inexpensive) project kickoff meeting?

We decided to at least try to quantify the value of holding an in-person project planning meeting, in particular a *kickoff* meeting, by doing a little research and combining that with some common sense and our experience as project managers and consultants.

The Importance of Building Trust

In a *Forbes* article, "Are Physical Meetings Becoming Outdated: Could Saving $10,000 Cost You $1M?" author Keld Jensen says that "trust is the glue that binds a business agreement." Why do we mention *trust*? And what's all this about a *business agreement*? Well, as we mentioned in our chapter on the importance of team building, a huge part of building a project team is trust. And since a project planning meeting is all about getting agreement on project goals, tasks, and a basic plan, a main outcome of the meeting is indeed a sort of business agreement.

What affects the levels of trust? Studies in the field of interpersonal communications have indicated that levels of trust are primarily influenced by *nonverbal communication* in better than 90 percent of the cases examined. A *Scientific American* article from Piercarlo Valdesolo (2013) indicates that the signals that yield trust in humans are mainly nonverbal, which was ironically with studies at Northeastern University involving, ironically, a robot.

At a project kickoff meeting, much of what takes place in terms of trust-building will occur not only at the meetings themselves but at coffee breaks, lunches, dinners, and other activities. This isn't trivial. Business psychologist Hazel Carter-Showell (Lennox 2013) found that social aspects such as small talk and sharing refreshments are an important part of client relationship building. She states, "They enable trust to be built through sharing commonalities and increased exposure to positive traits, such as predictability." Connecting on a level beyond task-oriented emails and phone calls will deepen the level of trust between parties, making for a more successful outcome. This intrigued us, so we contacted Carter-Showell, who contributed the following update:

A Meeting of Minds Revisited

Four years have passed since I researched international meeting behaviors to identify the top dos and don'ts of time, place, and interaction – whatever continent you find yourself meeting others on. In 2013, I found a remarkable consistency in the value of meeting in person, which is down to our brain chemistry. Whilst the best day for a meeting is cultural, the best time of day is not – as it is based on how our brains wake from sleep. Similarly, whilst greetings may vary with culture, the universal annoyance of colleagues checking emails did not. There is something deeply human about our need to really connect, to feel heard and to build trusting authentic relationships – which does not happen quickly or deeply without genuine human connection.

It takes more than an occasional video call to build trust, respect and lasting relationships – in business or out. Research suggests that trust is the foundation of high-performing teams, and the bedrock of interpersonal relationships. Since 2013, I have become fascinated by the neuroscience of trust. Particularly, how we generate trust through the words we choose and how we use them.

Judith E Glaser (in her 2013 book, *Conversational Intelligence*) synthesized aspects of neuroscience and linguistics to create the new discipline of conversational intelligence. This growing area of interest recognizes that the right words can trigger vital oxytocin in the brain required for bonding and trust, and the wrong ones can spike cortisol, the stress hormone.

What we now know is that most conversations are simply transactional, we tell, we sell, we ask questions we already know the answer to. Those types of meetings have the feeling of a well-known dance where everyone knows the steps – but no one innovates or feels they have true autonomy, so they sleepwalk through the meeting, checking their phone or fitness tracker to see how long until it's over. When conversations have this transactional feel, cortisol levels are usually high, participants act defensively to protect their own interest, and team dynamics flounder due to low trust.

At the other end of the spectrum is a group having a conversation using "we" more than "I" and asking questions they don't know the answer to – genuinely co-creating solutions with each other. In this style of conversation, participants recognize the trust that is shown and they feel involved in the solution. Oxytocin and trust are high, which, paradoxically, permits people to challenge each other healthily without fear that the relationship will be damaged.

In-person meetings allow the most effective levels of trust to be built by raising oxytocin. They are an investment of a finite resource – time – and we value what is not freely available. Showing that you invest in relationships says a great deal about you. In particular, that people matter more than profit. Putting customers and colleagues at the heart of thinking, doing nothing about them without them, puts meaning into meetings. Making the decision to not meet in person to cut costs reminds me of my favorite metaphor of putting on an opera without the music – you get the plot but not the point. Meeting without actually meeting conveys content but not connection. In a current study of successful entrepreneurs, I found that most believe the right deal is better than the best deal – and the right deal allows relationships to survive and thrive. This is a world away from the "greed is good" approach of the 1990s and emphasizes the growing recognition of the value and power of relationships.

In-person meetings also allow every subtle micro-expression or gesture to be read. These micro-signals form in 400 to 750 microseconds, but it takes a second to control your face to deceive or to hide an emotion – so there is always a quarter-second delay when the real feeling leaks. When negotiating, reading these signals can be vitally important, to know when to stop selling, stop talking, or simply stop the meeting – and when to hold or fold. Many video conferencing platforms have tiny delays or poor picture resolution, meaning this crucial information is lost. From frustrated toe tapping under the table to avoiding eye contact, or breathing changes as someone ends a point or winds up to make another– these are signals that are lost. These micro-expressions are how participants work out effective turn-taking to balance contribution in a meeting, allowing freer contribution and spontaneity while feeling respectful. On video or tele-conferences, more formal rules of engagement and contribution are required to prevent talking over each other, which can leave the meeting feeling transactional, not transformational.

Some introverts can find it challenging to break into a conversation, and a colleague reading their micro-gesture of intent or frustration can ease their way to join in. This explains how so many can spend entire virtual meetings in silence and no one notices. Similarly, extroverts can crash the end of other people's sentences in their enthusiasm to contribute, and need to watch for signs that others want to speak. This is possible in person, but it can make them unpopular participants on teleconferences. In-person meetings can be designed to accommodate personality differences more readily than online formats, and this can be enhanced by technology rather than by using technology to replace human interaction. Right now, real-time feedback of contribution, facial cues, emotion, and language choice is available; this could be used to help those who find social interaction challenging for whatever reason. Then perhaps relationships wouldn't need to be commoditized, with quantity valued over quality. Meetings can be true meetings of minds, without differences of language, culture, behavior, or brain chemistry dividing us. I look forward to frictionless meetings where my female language patterns and use of space, combined with my British reserve exacerbated by my inner scientist's tendency toward geekiness, or my complete inability to take things too seriously for too long are accommodated. I'm looking forward to my first telling off for bad behavior in a meeting by IBM's Watson. I'm imagining a world where our meeting preferences (including lighting, food, and layout) are linked to our fingerprint as we enter a meeting room.

But that's in the future; right now the art of relationship building is dying. The wrong layers in organizations are let go, transactional exchanges are substituted. I had the same High Street bank manager for over a decade – he came for coffee and awkward but endearing small talk. When they replaced him with someone I didn't know, and they tried to make it sound like it was for my benefit in a standard letter that didn't even let him say goodbye, I left our bank of eighteen years to bank with one of the smaller private banks, where they actually talk to me, celebrate our company birthday with us, and meet me to talk regional economics, gossip, and sometimes about my business. But I knew I could trust my banker as soon as I met him, and yes, yes, yes, I do know about first impressions and the perceptual system. But he kept popping in – trust turning to liking, so now I have a bank manager I genuinely like, who seems interested in my business. His meetings must be oxytocin superfood because everyone I meet says the same thing – he takes the time to get to know you and will always pop over if you want a meeting.

To quote Simon Sinek, one of the most popular TED speakers ever, "We call a business a company – because it is a collection of people in the company of other people. It's the company that matters." All in all, if budget and time permit, human beings are, and will remain, ultra-social. I don't care how you get there – get to that meeting if you can!

The Project Management Institute (2017) also acknowledges this, saying, "Face-to-face interaction is usually the most effective way to build the trusting relationships that are needed to manage knowledge."

Returning to our earlier points on non-verbal cues, body language and physical reactions are important aspects of decision-making and relationship building for many business people. Carter-Showell also found that the most important elements to build trust are eye contact and reading nonverbal cues. "We can tell a smile is genuine because it reaches the eyes. The muscles by our mouths are under conscious control, but the muscles that crinkle the eyes and pull down the center of the eye brows are only activated when we smile genuinely," she said.

Selling the Project

Think of a kickoff meeting as an opportunity to sell the project to the core team contributors. This isn't much of a stretch. As a project manager or project sponsor you're above all else an influencer – a salesperson – so a project team meeting is, at least in some respects, a sales meeting. If you'll buy that (pun intended) you realize that selling is something best done *in person*. You'll also realize that you want to read your audience, and that's difficult to do in a virtual situation. In her *Forbes* article on why the best salespeople read body language, Carol Kinsey Goman (2015) advises you to focus on pupil size, the upper torso, and even the feet when reading your customer (in our case, your project team). That's hard to do even if you have top-of-the-line videoconference equipment with 4K quality, and it certainly isn't happening with instant messaging, even with prolific and expert use of smiley/frowny face emoticons.

Trying to Put a Number on It

Keld Jensen's *Forbes* article boldly claimed that saving $10,000 could cost you $1M. How could we even approach a number like this? Well, one study – admittedly done by a hotel company (IHG 2013), which would gain from more physical meetings does provide some potential for putting price tags on the physical meeting's worth. In a survey of over 2,000 business professionals across five major markets – the United Kingdom, the United States, the United Arab Emirates, China, and India, they found:

- Nearly half (47 percent) surveyed believe they had lost a contract or client because they didn't have enough face-to-face meetings, which resulted in an estimated yearly revenue loss of 24 percent – a significant loss for any business.

- Most respondents (81 percent) stated that face-to-face meetings are *better* for building long-term trust and ensuring strong client relationships.

- Yet, a majority (63 percent) reported that the number of virtual meetings they attended has increased in the past five to ten years, further demonstrating that the value of face-to-face meetings is being overlooked in favor of cost- and time-saving technologies, such as videoconferencing.

Clearly the cost of not holding in-person meetings can be significant.

Conclusion

We feel that, at least for your initial meetings, you should set the stage, build trust, and establish and maintain project team relationships with in-person meetings. Then, if possible (and depending on the length of the project), have in-person meetings to account for changes in team makeup or shifts in project scope, or to tackle difficult project issues. Other, less important meetings could be in-person, hybrid, or virtual.

APPENDIX A

Project Management Refresher

Based on *A Guide to the Project Management Body of Knowledge (PMBOK® Guide), Sixth Edition* by the Project Management Institute (PMI)

IF YOU'RE NEW TO PROJECT MANAGEMENT, need a refresher, or just want to expand your vocabulary, this Appendix is for you. We're going to use the analogy of an orchestra, with the project manager (you) as the conductor.

But before we go any further, let's go to the *PMBOK® Guide* (Project Management Institute 2017) for the definition of a project: "A project is a temporary endeavor undertaken to create a unique product, service, or result." Keep that word *unique* in mind. It's going to come back to help (and haunt) us later.

With this definition of a project in mind, as the conductor you need knowledge, skills, and certain attributes (talents) to conduct a concert (a temporary endeavor undertaken to create a unique result). Let's call these KSAs (knowledge, skills, and attributes). Those KSAs fall into two categories, what we'll call the art and the science of project management, which, in line with our analogy, we outline as follows:

The Art

- An ability to lead and inspire people
- Related to the above, an intangible charisma – displayed by an ability to read the audience and the mood of the orchestra

167

♦ Knowing the capabilities (strengths and weaknesses) of the various orchestra sections (for example, woodwinds) and individual players

The Science

♦ Virtuosity in at least one instrument, and knowledge of a vast array of instrument types

♦ Technical excellence in conducting

♦ Knowledge of music theory

♦ Ability to read music and knowledge of the science of harmonics, pacing, timing

The project manager (conductor), in directing the project, (concert), must lead the team (orchestra) through the following Project Management Process Groups from *A Guide to the Project Management Body of Knowledge, (PMBOK® Guide), Sixth Edition.*

♦ Initiating Process Group

♦ Planning Process Group

♦ Executing Process Group

♦ Monitoring and Controlling Process Group

♦ Closing Process Group

These five Process Groups, which some people incorrectly call phases, are groups of related processes, which overlap and intersect in many ways. Let's look at the overlap between the Executing Process Group and the Monitoring and Controlling Process Group. As you execute a project, you're also monitoring and controlling it. As our conductor, when you wave that wand, you're watching, listening, processing, and reacting to things such as volume, audience reaction, or a violinist dropping her bow. In short, you're looking at (monitoring) the difference between *planned* and *actual* (we call this *variance*) and adjusting (controlling) as necessary. Of course, it's not all reactive. Much of the response to the differences comes from planning. We'll cover this later when we discuss project risk management. In any case, you can see that there's a great deal of overlap and interaction here.

168

But let's go back to the Process Groups and give you our high-level, fast-forward refresher of project management.

Initiation

Here your focus is on the *inception* of the project. We assume that at this point the senior managers have chosen this particular project as having lasting benefit to the organization, and that the project is tied to the strategic mission, vision, and values of the enterprise. In our orchestra analogy, we wouldn't have you launch a new airliner. That's not part of the portfolio of your symphony organization. Nor would we have you lead the orchestra in a Greatest Hits of the Rolling Stones concert at a Handel and Hayden Society fundraiser. A rationale and business case have already justified the project, and this is where the senior managers hand off the project to you, a project manager.

Your assignment as the project manager is carried out with a key document called the *project charter*. This document contains a high-level description of what the project is all about, and it serves as a source of authority for you. As the conductor you would now have a license to conduct this piece of music. Since project managers are often in organizations that contain larger vertical organizations (silos) of functions, such as Software Development, Testing, Marketing, and Technical Support, you would put together a team (orchestra) that cuts horizontally through those silos. As our conductor you would cut through the silos of woodwinds, percussion, strings, and brass, having them provide a terrific performance – in perfect harmony.

In many organizations, one of the talents that a project manager needs is to influence without the official authority that may come with a much higher level or grade within the organization. The charter provides that source of authority. The other key process in *initiation* is the identification of *stakeholders*. This is key! If we don't know who is invested in the project, who is affected in any way, or who could cause the project to screech to a halt, we're setting ourselves up for failure. A stakeholder is a broad term in project management, applied to you, the team members, the functional managers, the customers or clients of your project's outcome (service or product) – anyone who cares, or may eventually care, about the project or its outcome.

Planning

One very short but important word comes to mind for all of the planning processes. That word is *how*. The key behind a successful project is good planning. You'll need to know, in advance, how resources will be used, how you'll communicate, how you'll procure, how you'll schedule, how you'll identify and respond to risk, how you'll deal with change, with constraints, with issues, with stakeholders . . . it's quite an extensive list.

Just under half, twenty four, of the forty-nine processes in PMI's *PMBOK® Guide, Sixth Edition*, are dedicated to planning. PMI calls for the creation of a Project Management Plan, which is *not* a Gantt chart, *not* a schedule, *not* a budget, but rather a wide-ranging collection of subsidiary plans, such as a Communications Management Plan, a Risk Management Plan, a Procurement Management Plan, and so on. Will you find lots of specifics in these plans, such as the key list of risks, or the detailed communications of the project? No. However, what you will find is the reasoning behind, and the logic of, and the structure for such project artifacts, the tools and records that will become the daily grind for the project manager. In the real world you may not find the formal Project Management Plan, but we have seen it implemented in an electronic format in some companies.

Executing

This is where you'll manage the day-to-day work of the project. PMI calls this Direct and Manage Project Work. In our orchestra analogy, you, as conductor, are waving your wand, turning pages of the score, encouraging one section (perhaps that lazy woodwind section) to play at the proper volume at a particular stanza in the performance. In our home-building case study, this is where you as the project manager would be overseeing deliverables and meeting objectives, such as Foundation Ready, Frame Complete, Electrical System Tested, and so on.

The bottom line is, even though Planning is where the project success is mostly determined, it's the Executing processes where the stereotypical project management work takes place. When a project manager comes home from work, if she's asked about her day, it's most likely that she'll discuss the project's execution.

Monitoring and Controlling

Remember we talked about that lazy woodwind section, and how you, the conductor, needed to get them to play loudly enough? Let's use that example to illustrate how Executing and Monitoring and Controlling overlap. You reach the stanza in which the woodwinds are supposed to pipe up (pun intended). There's an expected volume level (the plan) at that moment. You're listening (monitoring) for that planned volume. If the woodwinds come through and play at that level, as they did in re-hearsal, that's great, and you can continue unabated. If, however, due to any number of things (acoustics, stage fright, Clara the clarinetist having a bad day) the volume is too low, you will correct this with the appropriate waves of your wand. This is the controlling piece of Monitoring and Controlling – and three steps, executing, monitoring, and controlling, are taking place simultaneously.

Closing

The Closing processes center around putting the final wrapping on the project. In our orchestra analogy, you'd probably be tempted to think of closing as a stirring crescendo, a gong, and a rousing standing ovation. And that is part of Closing, but not all of it, by any stretch. You, and the orchestra members, are taking note (again, pun intended) of what worked, what didn't, things to avoid in the future, and things that are worth repeating in later performances.

Once again, these lessons learned are best recorded as they happen so the history is freshly remembered. If we leave the orchestra and return to typical projects, what we're prescribing is simply this: record, preserve, and share lessons learned for future projects. If you're in a larger orga-nization, make sure that these are widely shared for use by the project managers of your community. And make sure you do this for project planning meetings in particular. Indeed, a major theme of this book is to share with you lessons we and other seasoned project managers have learned so that you can take advantage of this (dare we say) wisdom.

Knowledge Areas

Let's leave the realm of Process Groups and delve into some fundamentals that come from the Knowledge Areas, which are identified areas of project management that are used in most projects most of the time. There are ten of them:

- Project Integration Management
- Project Scope Management
- Project Schedule Management
- Project Cost Management
- Project Quality Management
- Project Resource Management
- Project Communications Management
- Project Risk Management
- Project Procurement Management
- Project Stakeholder Management

Since this is a refresher and not a graduate-level course, we won't provide a comprehensive overview but will instead highlight the most helpful concepts.

Let's start with one of the most fundamental and yet often misunderstood concepts of project management – scope. We define scope as what's in and what's not in the project's work. That means we have to consider not only product scope – the features and functionality of the product, service, or outcome we're providing – but also project scope, by which we mean the work elements and deliverables it will take to deliver that product scope.

For example, let's say you're the project manager for a fundraiser that involves baking ten cakes for sale at a charity bake sale. It's obvious that your product scope will include flour, water, sugar, eggs, and frosting. Further, you can easily imagine that utensils and appliances will be needed to prepare the cake, and a recipe needs to be available to guide the team through the process. However, how about the fact that your team of cake-bakers will perform more cheerily (think Snow White and the Seven Dwarfs . . . Whistle While You Work) if there's some peppy music playing in the background? If you buy this idea, then an MP3 player and a small audio system may be part of the scope of this project. How are the cakes being transported? If the project includes getting the cakes to some central location, then this, too, becomes part of project scope. How about cleanup? Does the project include leaving the room the way you found it?

Determining scope is so fundamental because, if an element of scope (project or product) is left out initially, there will be no schedule, people, resources, or money allocated to it, no risks identified for it, no communications planned for it – all of these things will have to be haphazardly thrown at this element of scope at the last minute.

In our cake-baking example, someone will have to run home to grab their music system or perhaps get cleaning materials that were not properly identified as part of scope. These last-minute pieces of scope are disruptive, annoying, and may potentially affect the morale of the team as well as its efficiency and effectiveness.

The Triple Constraint

This brings us to the topic of constraints. The triple constraint, consisting of scope, time, and cost, is a fundamental principle of project management. The three constraints are interdependent: None of them can be altered without affecting one or both of the others. Rather than use the common two-dimensional triangle to represent the interdependencies of these three constraints, we use a three-dimensional triangle – a pyramid (technically a tetrahedron). The walls of the tetrahedron are scope, cost, and time, and the floor is the project's risk and uncertainty (due to its uniqueness). The fabric of the walls, and the contents of the object, represent quality – delivering what the customer asked for. (See Exhibit A.1)

The walls are *interdependent*. An increase in scope is likely going to mean a longer timeline and a bigger budget. A budget cut will likely cause a reduction of scope and a delay in the timeline. A compressed schedule will likely cause more money to be spent (think overtime) and may also cause you to trim scope. In more casual terms, it's difficult to have a project that's fast, cheap, *and* good. It's a balancing act. And you, the project manager – the conductor – are at the apex of this pyramid,

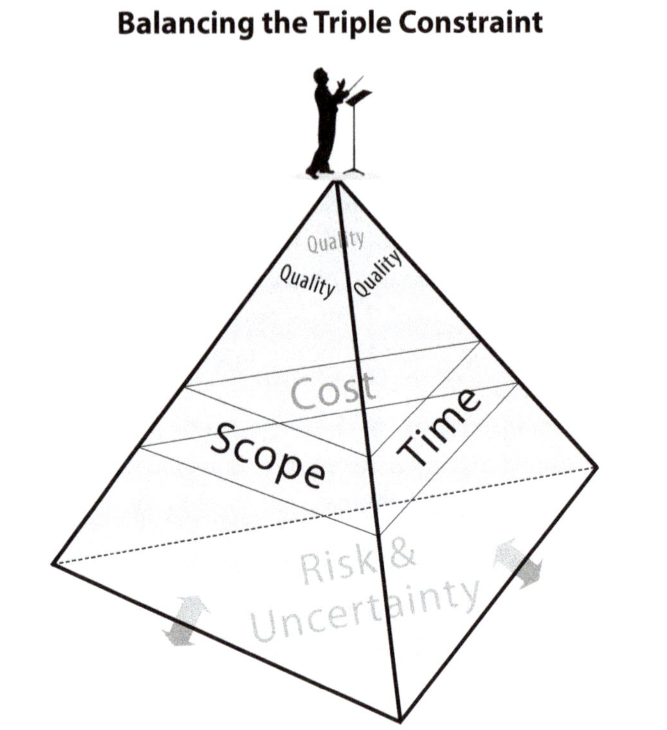

Balancing the Triple Constraint

Exhibit A.1. One of the project manager's jobs Is to balance the triple constraint – scope, schedule, and cost (with quality added) – to have a successful project.

trying to balance scope, schedule, and budget, all with a very unsteady floor that's resting on unstable ground (risk).

The General Order of Things: Scope, Schedule, Cost

Here are some ways in which we can deal with the interdependencies of these constraints. One guiding principle is to always remember that they flow in this general planning sequence: scope, then schedule, and then and only then, cost. You determine what is in product and project scope before you can know how long the contributing tasks take, and the order of those tasks as well as their precedence. It's only then, when you do know the schedule, that you can properly plan costs. For example, you need to know how many framers have to be at the work site on which days (including weekends, perhaps) before you can accurately estimate a budget.

Ranking the Constraints

Most project management books will focus on the triple constraint (classically, scope, time, and cost, or alternatively, quality, schedule, and budget). What's important for you to remember as a project manager and as a team facilitator, is that the relative importance of each of these must be consciously chosen and kept in view of the team throughout the project. For example: For the Panama Canal (a project whose outcome is very clear – a pathway through the isthmus of Panama), the constraint of scope is number one. In other words, even if the canal is very inexpensive and comes in on time, it doesn't matter if it doesn't go all the way through. Your job as a project manager is to keep this relative ranking ever-present in the project team culture.

Scope Tools

Let's zoom in on the constraint of scope, with an emphasis on tools.

The Work Breakdown Structure

The single most important, and yet often overlooked, tool in all of project management is the WBS. It's important because it's the foundation of everything else to come in terms of planning tools. No WBS, no Gantt chart, no schedule, no responsibility assignment matrix, no possibility of a complete risk register, and, likely, with no WBS, lots of scope creep sprinkled with poor project team morale.

Scope Creep

No treatment of scope could be complete without touching on scope creep. This is the insidious trickle of new scope we have unconsciously let slip into the project. Without stringent and conscious control over what new scope is admitted into the project, scope creep translates into complexity, longer schedules, budget overruns, and often other intangibles such as poor team morale. As a facilitator of project team meetings, your job is to assure that any scope that's brought into the project is done

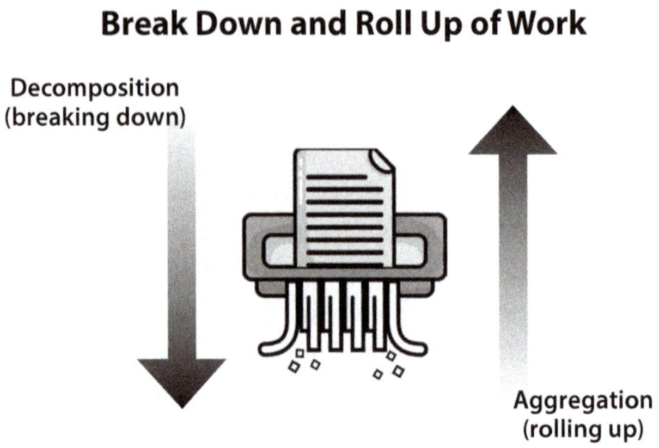

Break Down and Roll Up of Work

Exhibit A.2. The WBS breaks down work into tasks or rolls up work into sub-deliverables.

so consciously and with an agreed-upon, well-known methodology.

Strictly speaking, there's no reason you cannot add scope. But the Project Management Institute (2017) defines scope creep as, "The uncontrolled expansion to product or project scope without adjustment to time, scope, or resources." The key word there is *uncontrolled*. If controlled, by means of a change request/change control board system, you can make changes to scope and still keep the project in check.

The WBS is a picture of what's in the project. It shows, either in hierarchical form or in outline form, workstreams of tasks (work packages) that aggregate (roll up) to sub-deliverables (internal wiring completed) or major deliverables (electrical work completed) – see Exhibit A.2. To come back to our symphonic analogy, the WBS is not only the score of the piece of music, but the logistics for advertising the concert, setting up and tuning the instruments, even making sure that Harry the prima donna bassist gets that particular meal he needs before each performance.

Exhibit A.3 shows an image of a simple WBS. Chapter 9 illustrates how to create one.

The Scope Statement

The scope statement is a narrative version of the WBS and project charter, including key items such as:

Simple Work Breakdown Structure

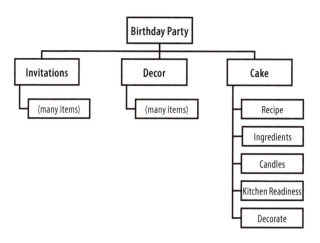

Exhibit A.3. A simple work breakdown structure for a birthday party.

- Rationale for selection of this project and link to organizational strategy
- Scope description
- High-level project requirements
- Project boundaries (including handover/handoff info)
- Project strategy
- High-level project deliverables
- Acceptance criteria
- Project constraints (including priority)
- Project assumptions (important for identifying risk)
- Cost estimates

Schedule Management

Once, and only after, the work has been decomposed into tasks and we know all of the tasks that make up 100 percent of the project work, we can start to understand the time dimension of our project. The key to understanding this facet of project management is recognizing that we now need to look at the attributes of tasks that affect timing, such as:

- The duration of each task

- The dependencies that exist between tasks

- Where there can be (or should be) overlap between tasks

- Resource limitations that could affect whether it's possible to do a task at an appointed time

- Lag and lead times due to physics or regulations (for example, time for a building's cement foundation to harden)

In our symphony performance, the conductor needs to know that a rousing fanfare takes pace only after that clarinet solo by Karen (allowing for applause, because she is *amazing*).

In this refresher we cannot go into the details but, below are some important concepts to know.

The Network Diagram and the Critical Path

As mentioned above, many project tasks will be dependent on others. This defines a logic, connecting the tasks together, with arrows representing the dependencies. In the simple diagram in Exhibit A.4, we show five tasks, A though E, with dependencies indicated by arrows and the duration of each task on the rectangle that represents the task. This is called a network diagram. If we walk through this diagram from start to finish using all possible routes, we can find a longest path through the network – in this case Start-A-C-D-E-End . This longest path through the network is also the shortest time in which the project can be completed, as defined by these dependencies. That critical path has no float (also called slack). Float is the amount of time that a task can slip without delaying the project's end date. Using these two definitions together, we can see that this means that if any of the tasks on the critical path slip, even by one hour, the project's completion will be delayed by one hour.

Let's take a moment to clarify a common misconception here. The tasks on our critical path are not any more important than the other tasks. They are time critical, but not any more important. Remember – by definition, if it's in the WBS, it's important to the project. Here we're

Network Diagram Showing the Critical Path

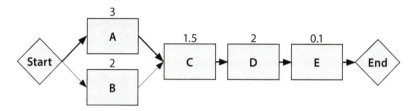

Critical Path = Start-A-C-D-E-End = 3 + 1.5 + 2 + 0.1 = 6.6 hours

Task	Task Code	Duration (hrs.)	Predecessor
Start	Milestone	0	
Obtain recipe and ingredients	A	1	Start
Obtain candles	B	2	Start
Bake cake	C	1.5	A and B
Frost cake and insert candles	D	2	C
Light candles	E	0.1	D
End	Milestone	0	E

Exhibit A.4. The critical path is the longest path through the network and also the shortest time in which the project can be completed.

looking only at time criticality. These tasks are indeed critical if you're looking to compress the schedule – to bring the end date in earlier. Through critical path analysis we can find ways to rearrange resources to possibly do just that. Again, that's beyond the scope of this refresher; see our references for some excellent guides with detailed discussions of critical path analysis, forward and backward pass calculations, and so on.

Cost and Procurement Management

Let's touch on a few key concepts and tools regarding the related Knowledge Areas of Cost and Procurement Management. One main concept is

Cumulative Spend Over Time

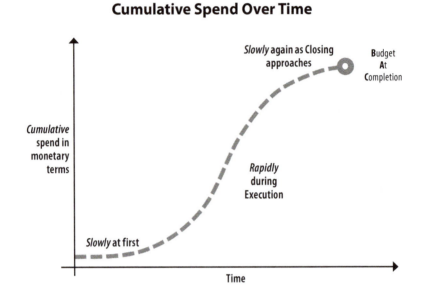

Exhibit A.5. An S-curve is used to show the cumulative spend over time.

the idea of a budget. Since a project is a unique, time-limited endeavor that consumes resources, it needs an overall budget as well as the time-phased component that shows us how the money will be spent as we move through the lifecycle of the project. Resources (we'll revert to *money* for the rest of this discussion) are expended slowly at first, then much more quickly during the execution of the project, and then slowly again as we approach the end date of the project. This yields the classic S-curve that results when we plot cumulative spend of money over the life of the project (see Exhibit A.5).

There's an entire field of study around earned value management that's beyond the scope of this refresher, but suffice it to say that if you carefully track a few key attributes – earned value, planned value, and actual costs – not only can you quantify key variances and indexes with respect to your spending rate and accomplishment of project work, you can also make forecasts as to whether or not (and by how much) you will be over or under budget, and whether or not, and by how much, you'll be late (or early).

Worth noting for this refresher is that the PV (planned value) curve represents the budget baseline. Remember our discussion of scope creep above? Establishing and communicating this baseline, and re-baselining when conscious scope acceptance has occurred through a formal process, is the key to avoiding significant overspends in your project. This could be a key tool for you, the facilitator, to use to convey this important message in a recurring way.

Risk

For this refresher we only want to familiarize (or re-familiarize) you with key concepts and tools from the Knowledge Area called Project Risk Management. First and foremost, here is the definition of project risk (Project Management Institute 2017): "An uncertain event, which, if it occurs, has a positive or negative effect on one or more project objectives."

Wait, what? Did that definition just allow for something called *positive risk*? Indeed, it does. Positive risk, which is also called *opportunity*, is the chance that something good happens to your project. In our symphony example, let's say that Tamara, our flute soloist, has quit a week ago and you have a replacement. As it turns out, Kavita is *far superior to Tamara*. Boom (or rather toot): an opportunity.

Of course, the dominant type of risk is not opportunity but threat. This is the chance that something that will affect a project objective in a negative way occurs. So in our example, Tamara quits disruptively in the middle of her solo. This affects a project objective – to have a performance uninterrupted by self-inflicted drama.

As a facilitator you're going to be responsible for identifying risk. But here's a tip: you can have your team identify all of the things that could go horrifically wrong, and flip them to opportunities by asking "what if" questions. And, you can identify things that can go tremendously well, and flip them as well to help tease out threats.

Estimation

Project managers must often estimate attributes of tasks or of the entire project. Mainly it all boils down to estimating durations (time/schedule) and cost (budget). There's an entire science of estimation beyond the scope of this refresher, but it's incumbent on the project manager to know a bit about estimation principles and techniques.

First and foremost, the project needs to avoid taking point estimates at face value. If a vendor claims that it will take three weeks to get something done, don't simply write down 3.0 weeks in your schedule. Since this task is in the future, it's by definition open to uncertainty – it could be possibly be completed in one week, if you're lucky, or in eleven weeks if things go haywire.

One technique to consider is the PERT three-point estimate, in which we push back on the vendor and ask not only for a most-likely (ML) three-week estimate but also a pessimistic (P) eleven-week estimate and an optimistic (O) one-week estimate. We use all three points, giving a weight of four votes to the most likely estimate. The weighted PERT estimate then is $(O + [4 \times ML] + P)/6$, in this case four weeks. Not only is that four weeks a more intelligent estimate, when we ask the vendor what makes it possible to accelerate their deliverable (for the optimistic estimate), we identify opportunities, and when we ask them what could delay their deliverable (for the pessimistic estimate), we identify threats. The PERT (Program Evaluation and Review Technique) three-point estimate was developed by the U.S. Navy for their Polaris missile project, which had a great deal of uncertainty.

Quality

A full treatment of quality management principles is beyond the scope of this refresher. See our references for some excellent resources on managing project quality. However, we do want to point out that it's important for project managers to be familiar with key quality concepts. After all, since a project is about transforming an idea to reality, the project manager needs to fully understand the drivers behind that idea, the requirements that that idea has brought to the project, a means to measure whether or not the project itself is operating with quality, and whether the product of the project (interim products and/or its final outcome or deliverable) are meeting the requirements set forth at the project's outset.

Distinguishing Project and Product Quality

The Project Management Institute (2017) defines *quality* as, "The degree to which a set of inherent characteristics fulfills requirements." For the subject of this book, then, quality is the degree to which a project kickoff meeting fulfills the requirements of our project kickoff meeting. For a house, or bridge, or app, quality is the degree to which the house, bridge, or app fulfills the requirements we established at the project's start (and with any approved changes, of course).

APPENDIX B

Project Management and Facilitation Certifications

Project Management Institute Certifications

PMI's PMP

The Project Management Professional (PMP) certification offered by the Project Management Institute is hugely popular. As of this writing there are about 815,000 PMP certifications. It's widely accepted because it includes not only a knowledge-based assessment, but it has a pre-requisite of three years of project management experience and thirty-five hours of project management training. This claimed experience and education is also heavily audited .

The certification also requires an exam – a four-hour, 200-question, multiple-choice exam, which is notoriously difficult and challenging. It requires preparation because PMI is looking for you to indicate that you understand the *PMBOK® Guide* framework and vocabulary. Of the four answers to choose from for each question in the exam, there are often several correct answers. Your task is to select the most correct and best answer. The questions are highly situational and test what you would do under certain circumstances based on the *PMBOK® Guide*.

Many companies in varied industries use the PMP as an intake requirement for project managers, and the processes and knowledge areas that are taught in preparation for the exam have been integrated into the work that's done by the project managers in these companies. The PMP is only one of a family of certifications offered by PMI, but it's the most prolific.

If you think you'd like the PMP certification, but you don't have the prerequisite three years of experience, PMI has provided an entry-level certification called the Certified Associate in Project Management (CAPM), which is similar to the PMP except that it doesn't require the aspect of leading and directing projects in the experience portion of the application. It requires a three-hour, 150-question exam and either 1,500 hours of professional experience on a project team or 23 contact hours of formal education.

Other PMI certifications are:

- **Program Management Professional (PgMP)** for those who have proven ability to oversee programs – collections of related projects managed together for benefits not available if managed separately

- **Portfolio Management Professional (PfMP)** for those who have proven ability to oversee large collections of projects, programs, and operations

- **PMI Scheduling Professional (PMI-SP)** for those with advanced knowledge and experience developing, managing and maintaining project schedules

- **PMI Risk Management Professional (PMI-RMP)** for those with advanced knowledge and experience in project risk management

- **PMI Agile Certified Practitioner (PMI-ACP)** for those with advanced knowledge and experience in agile project management

- **PMI Professional in Business Analysis (PMI-PBA)** for those with advanced knowledge and experience in business analysis

International Project Management Association Certifications

The IPMA Four-Level Certification (4-L-C) System

IPMA, like PMI, offers internationally recognized certifications. It has certified over 150,000 individuals globally. Please note that the IPMA is an organization that has more local oversight and less central oversight than PMI, so if you're curious about these certifications you should refer to www.ipma.world/certification/certification-bodies/ to find the appropriate certification body for your country. For example, in the United States, the certification body can be found at www.ipma-usa.org.

IPMA certifications are advertised as being competence-based rather than knowledge-based, and they align with their Individual Competence Baseline (ICB4). Learn more at www.ipma-usa.org/icb4. That said, the PMP tends to be the more marketable certification, at least in the United States.

IPMA provides four individual certifications for varying levels of experience, complexity, and contribution:

- ◆ **IPMA Level A.** Certified Projects Director for those who lead complex project portfolios and programs. A peer review and assessment is performed.

- ◆ **IPMA Level B.** Certified Senior Project Manager for those who lead complex projects – this requires five years of experience as a pre-requisite. An oral case study is required.

- ◆ **IPMA Level C.** Certified Project Manager for those who lead projects of moderate complexity – this requires a minimum of three years of experience. Its exam consists of essay questions.

- ◆ **IPMA Level D.** Certified Project Management Associate for individuals who apply project management knowledge when working on projects. Its exam consists of multiple choice plus essay questions.

PRINCE2 Certifications

PRINCE2 is an acronym for PRojects IN Controlled Environments. It's a standard project management methodology used extensively in the United Kingdom, other European markets, and Australia (there is rapid worldwide growth as well). It's overseen by a governing body known as AXELOS, which is a joint venture company, created in 2013 by the Cabinet Office on behalf of Her Majesty's Government in the United Kingdom and Capita plc, to manage, develop, and grow their global best practice portfolio.

PRINCE2 certification requires no project management experience, unlike the PMP and IPMA (both of which require at least three years of prior project management experience). PRINCE2 training (required) and the Foundation and Practitioner Exams are entirely in English, as well as exam prep materials and study guides. One important difference, and probably a point in favor of the exam, is that PRINCE2 certification is entirely methodology-based, where the PMP is knowledge-based and IPMA is competence-based.

PRINCE2 was established by the U.K. government to specify a methodology for doing projects. Contrast that with PMI's *PMBOK® Guide*, on which most of the PMP exam questions are based. The *PMBOK® Guide* provides a framework and a vocabulary for managing projects, but it does not prescribe how to run them. PRINCE2 does. Because of this, the PRINCE2 preparation process is lengthy and arduous, but clearly not impossible – over a million people have some form of PRINCE2 certification.

There are two main levels of PRINCE2 certification – Foundation and Practitioner. The Foundation level introduces the PRINCE2 method. The Foundation certification aims to confirm that you know and understand the PRINCE2 method well enough to be able to work effectively with, or as a member of, a project management team working within an environment supporting PRINCE2.

The Foundation certification also serves as a prerequisite for the Practitioner certification. The Practitioner level certification is for those managing projects as part of their role. This could be as part of a formal project management function or a role in which project management is an inherent part of day-to-day work. The purpose of the Practitioner certification is to confirm that you have sufficient understanding of how to apply the PRINCE2 methodology in multiple project environments. There are PRINCE2 Practitioner and PRINCE2 Agile Practitioner certifications.

The International Institute for Facilitation Certifications

While reading a *Harvard Business Review* article (Basu and Savani 2017), it didn't surprise me to learn that "people who viewed options together, selected the best option more often than those who viewed options individually. We also found that compared with those who viewed options one at a time, people who viewed options together used more phrases suggesting deep thought (e.g., "I *think* X is more than Y" or "*Hence*, I feel Y is the correct option")."

These finding are a solid reminder of the benefits gained when:

◆ Groups work well together

◆ A person uses facilitation skills to help a group develop options and outcomes

◆ Appropriate decision-making tools and processes are used with groups

Whether you formally facilitate as a neutral facilitator or you use facilitative skills (perhaps as a leader, instructor, or when working with groups), it's worth knowing what makes a good facilitator.

The International Institute for Facilitation (INIFAC) surveyed 450 facilitators and clients on what makes a good facilitator. The results formed the basis for the development of a quantifiable facilitator certification that comprises quality, integrity, breadth, and rigor. "We want a credential that facilitators and those using facilitative skills can aspire to. We also want a credential that clients can depend on," was the goal of INIFAC's founders.

Based on a set of six facilitator competency areas (formed out of the original survey), the Certified Master Facilitator (CMF) was created. This credential is intended to distinguish a person as having achieved the highest certification level available in the industry.

The assessment process covers *knowledge* (through a written assessment), *skills* (through a virtual performance assessment/video role-play), and *experience* (through an experience review and client references).

The Competencies of a Certified Master Facilitator

There are six competencies and thirty sub-competencies that define a CMF.

1. **Presence.** CMFs bring compassion and authority to the room. Through their verbal and nonverbal expression, they exude confidence, energy, and self-awareness while also conveying a high

level of warmth and caring. They make adjustments in their style to better serve the group.

2. **Assessment.** CMFs know and ask the questions necessary to accurately assess a client need. Based on their learning from past experiences, they create processes designed to address the client's specific requirements. They carefully plan and prepare sessions. They recognize when a planned process is not working effectively and are able to define alternative processes quickly to reach the desired outcome.

3. **Communication.** CMFs are skilled communicators. They actively listen, making sure to playback and confirm important points. They have highly-tuned analytic skills which allow them to process information quickly, differentiate various content issues and isolate critical points in a discussion. They ask questions that help groups to engage effectively. They deliver instructions that are accurate, clear and concise. They effectively identify and verbally summarize agreements.

4. **Control.** CMFs create and maintain a productive and safe environment in which participants with diverse styles and cultures can engage in interactions that stay focused on achieving the goal. They maintain control of the session and an appropriate pace. They understand causes of disagreement and can effectively guide a group through conflict. They consciously take action to prevent, detect, and resolve dysfunctional behavior.

5. **Consistency.** CMFs understand and consistently apply best practice techniques for such activities as starting the session, focusing the group, recording information, and closing the session.

6. **Engagement.** CMFs know and use multiple techniques for engaging a group, problem solving, decision-making, promoting creativity, and raising energy.

INIFAC also offers a Certified Competent Facilitator certification for those with less experience. If you are interested in becoming a CMF or CCF or in learning more about these marks of excellence in facilitation profession, visit INIFAC's website at www.inifac.org.

Other Certifications: Caveat Emptor

There are other certifications out there. We urge you to research these carefully. Some use organization and certificate names which emulate the names above, and charge similar or higher amounts for certification but are not issued by well-recognized, industry-standard bodies such as IPMA, PMI, AXELOS or INIFAC.

For all of the certifications discussed above, we highly recommend that you go directly to the certifying agency to get the latest information, since the certifications (and the prerequisites, and the exams) are subject to change.

Brainstorm to Generate and Highlight to Narrow

Teresa Lawrence, PhD, PMP, CSM

L INUS PAULING, WINNER OF BOTH A NOBEL PRIZE IN CHEMISTRY and the Nobel Peace Prize, said, "If you want to have good ideas you must have many ideas." This is the cornerstone of brainstorming! When we brainstorm, we're going for ideas – lots and lots of ideas!

As part of the creative problem-solving process, brainstorming is one of many divergent thinking tools that help project teams generate novel and useful ideas. Divergent thinking is a process for generating ideas and solutions only. I say *only* because in divergent thinking, ideas aren't discussed, developed, or decided upon; ideas are simply generated and collected. When the time comes to discuss, develop, or decide, savvy project teams know to make the shift into convergent thinking. Think about it – just as a driver cannot accomplish anything by accelerating and braking at the same time, project management teams cannot find ideal solutions by coming up with ideas and judging them at the same time.

There are four key principles that make divergent thinking and divergent thinking tools work. When project teams commit to these principles, their thinking will shift smoothly to new possibilities beyond the obvious, and their behavior will demonstrate an openness to new ideas and new behavior.

The four principles of divergent thinking are:

1. **Defer all judgment of the ideas generated.** Remember, at this stage we're only generating ideas. Ideas don't go bad!

2. **Strive for quantity.** Consider setting an idea quota – how many ideas can you get in three minutes? A well-trained team of eight can easily come up with 100 ideas in less than five minutes.

3. **Make connections.** Piggyback and build on ideas shared by others.

4. **Seek novelty.** It's so much easier to tame a wild idea than to bring a boring one to life.

Invented by Alex Osborn in 1953, he defines brainstorming as "a group's attempt to find solutions for a specific problem by amassing ideas." Brainstorming is perhaps the purest form of divergent thinking. Before your team jumps into a brainstorming session, consider a warm-up first. A warm-up reminds team members of the principles, lets them practice the tool, and sets the climate. Warm-up activities always have a silly factor, and they're designed that way on purpose. Why? Because shifting the team to an imaginative and playful mindset will help them with idea generation when they approach the real problem they are tackling.

Good ideas for warm-ups often start with one of these lines:

◆ In what ways might we improve . . . a bathtub? Glove? Suitcase?

◆ How might we benefit from . . . 100,000 paper clips? 50,000 golf balls?

◆ How might you use . . . a paperclip? Plunger?

There are many variations to brainstorming ranging from having a scribe write down ideas to having team members share ideas in a Google Doc. One effective brainstorming tool is called Stick 'em Up Brainstorming. This tool works best when it's facilitated by someone other than a team member, since this ensures that everyone on the team is participating in the solution.

Stick 'em Up Brainstorming directions:

1. Review the divergent guidelines!

2. On large flipchart paper, write down the statement of the challenge that the team is working on. Be sure these can be seen by everyone.

3. Give every team member a stack of 3×5 sticky notes and a wide-tipped marker.

4. Set an idea quota.

5. Then, based on the challenge, when team members have an idea to contribute they *write* their idea on a sticky note, *say* their idea aloud, and *pass* their sticky note forward to the facilitator, who posts it on the chart paper. Saying the idea aloud triggers new ideas and encourages others to immediately expand or contribute to that idea.

6. One idea per sticky note.

7. No discussing ideas.

8. Every fifteen ideas or so, have the facilitator check in with a lead team member to be sure the ideas are headed in the right direct.

9. Don't stop until the idea quota has been met or the team has enough ideas to address the challenge.

This is often where teams stop, feeling proud of themselves for generating so many ideas and, at the same time, paralyzed about how to sort and select from among them. This isn't as hard as it seems! Convergent thinking shifts the focus to examining what's been created and on how and which ideas will be used. The goal in this process is to arrive at a short list of ideas that address the challenge. Just as there are principles for divergent thinking and generating ideas, there are principles for convergent thinking and choosing from among options.

The four principles of convergent thinking are:

1. **Apply affirmative judgement.** Carefully consider the strengths of the idea. What works and what do you like about the idea? Remember, most ideas aren't born perfect!

2. **Be open to novelty.** Entertain highly original options that you might otherwise eliminate, because they might lead to a breakthrough.

3. **Check your objectives.** Is the idea that you're exploring on track to solving the problem?

4. **Stay focused.** Invest the time to ensure that ideas are developed.

A useful tool in convergent thinking is called Highlighting. This tool helps teams narrow from many ideas to a few good options. It features three steps: hits, clustering, and restating.

1. Hits is straightforward and uses intuition to choose ideas that are especially interesting, promising, compelling, intriguing, innovative, or on-target.

2. Clustering organizes your hits into groups, categories, or themes. It's okay to allow unique data or ideas to stand alone.

3. Restating captures the essence of the cluster. Team members try to synthesize all the different options into one statement to capture the essence. The goal is to bring the cluster to life!

Here's how it works: Imagine that you have brainstormed and reviewed the principles for convergent thinking. Next, team members stand and, independently, review all the ideas generated. Using stickers or a check mark, team members identify ideas that pique their interest and have the potential to solve the problem. Then the group organizes the related stickered ideas into clusters (sound a little like affinity diagrams?). Finally, the team is asked to synthesize ideas in the clusters and to restate them into an overarching, elaborated idea. Typically, if there are more than ten ideas in a cluster, there's more than one theme present.

When project teams take time to separate divergent and convergent thinking and use tools such as brainstorming and highlighting, the chances of arriving at a novel and useful solution increase dramatically.

APPENDIX D

Meeting War Stories

From Various Authors

SOME PEOPLE HAVE A GREAT AVERSION TO PREDICTING DATES, especially in the face of uncertainty. One of us worked with a technical
person who was very capable in every other way, but whenever he was
faced with a schedule and needed to determine activities and dependencies, he could focus only on dates. No matter how hard we tried to assure
him that we were just looking for what it would take to get the work
done, he could only see those dates. The following (circular) conversation shows the dilemma this causes:

> *Date-Driven-Dave*: "We can't make it by the 25th."
>
> *My response*: "We know that, Dave. We're not asking you to com-
> mit to a date. The scheduling software automatically puts dates
> on. We just want to find out what the activities are and how long
> they'll take."
>
> *Date-Driven-Dave (after some grumbling and looking at the
> schedule)*: "We can't make it by the 25th."
>
> *(repeat chorus)*

In this instance we were able to defuse the date problem by putting
all the activities and dependencies in a spreadsheet. That allowed Dave to
focus on the what and not the when.

However, you may not have this luxury in your meeting since you must leave there with some idea of dates, however inexact. One way to deal with this is to hide the columns in your schedule that talk about dates. Then once you have the activities, you can add those columns back in and start focusing on dates.

Some team members may still have an issue with dates. But at this point you can say that you're going to factor in the assumptions and risks that may prevent getting to those dates. In other words, there *is* uncertainty and you're making allowances for it. Not only that, this is a draft schedule, and you'll be revisiting teams to make modifications and adjust for what they've learned since.

At some point in time, the schedule will need to be baselined, meaning that there's an agreed-upon start and end, which are also used for measurement. If people still cannot commit to dates, you may have a bigger problem to be solved. Remember – Brooks' law applies here – Adding human resources to a late software project makes it later. While the author, Fred Brooks, called it a gross oversimplification, he points to several factors that provide some truth to this law:

- It takes time for new people on a project to ramp up.
- Communication overheads increase as the number of people increases.
- Nine women can't make a baby in one month, but one woman can make a baby in nine months.

10 Kilos Lighter

One of our clients is project manager of a research team. He asked us to support him and his team to make the regular team meetings more effective. According to him the meetings took too much time and drained his energy, and discussions often took too long. Although he expected us to focus on the execution of the meeting itself, we spent a lot of time in helping him prepare the meeting: Which items are on the agenda? Why are they on the agenda? Who is the owner of this agenda item? What is the desired outcome of this agenda item according to the owner? And also: What do you expect from the members of your team? How should they prepare? What could you let them do instead of doing it all yourself? What would be a good process to handle each agenda item?

During the following meetings the project manager and his team learned the power of joint preparation, and they discovered the fun and effectiveness of applying different working formats during the meeting: standup brainstorming around a whiteboard, listening, and asking open questions of the owner of an agenda item instead of having lengthy discussions.

After the third meeting that we had attended the project manager come to me, smiling, and said, "I'm surprised what the team members can do and the commitment they show in making our collaboration more effective. It feels like a joint effort now instead of me doing all the work. I feel 10 kilos lighter than before!!"

The Gemstone

This kickoff meeting was a real nightmare. I had been summoned, suddenly and for the first time, to a meeting with the president of the firm and top management. The president had learned from his senior managers that I was doing a great job for his company, and he wanted to put me to the test. He asked me what I thought about some strategic projects that I knew very well. But there were new, unclear goals, budgets that weren't plausible, tight schedules, and limited resources. I told this to him frankly. He replied that all his senior managers agreed with him. He asked them to show me the latest reports and the last notes that they had prepared. They began to look for them, but there was confusion with the various documents and their various revisions. In all that disorder the president became angry. He insulted his senior managers. He screamed and beat his fists on the meeting table. A gemstone flew off his ring. He yelled even louder. I was shocked. Then I thought about it. Yes! His flaring temper caused his senior managers to shield him from the facts. Where were the senior managers? I didn't see them anymore. I looked under the meeting table. His senior managers were crawling on the floor looking for the president's gemstone. It was at that moment that I decided to resign.

Non-Verbal Communication

I had a final project meeting that was very challenging and rewarding. It was a civilian and military summit meeting, with representatives from the U.S. Congress. They were all very serious, formal, and obsequious. I recognized the Navy captain, the key stakeholder, for whom we had developed the project. Everyone saluted him with great respect and with a particular verbal form, which, as a contractor from Europe, I didn't know. It wasn't a language problem. I just didn't know how to say hello to a U.S. Navy captain in the official way. I couldn't avoid saying hello to him, because I knew him very well and we had often worked together.

While I was looking around thoughtfully, I met his eyes at the end of the huge meeting table and smiled at him. I simply *smiled*. He returned an equally friendly smile. I discovered the power of non-verbal communication.

The Bathroom Breaker

One of my project team representatives from a key organization didn't want to participate in the meeting. He would always excuse himself for a visit to the restroom and then be absent for the half hour in which he was supposed to contribute. This happened repeatedly. I spoke to him about this and he simply said, "When you gotta go, you gotta go." Since the one-on-one conversation failed to resolve the problem, I escalated it to his manager, who provided a representative with "a stronger stomach" – and the meetings proceeded with full contribution and no long-term bathroom breaks.

Very Proper and Very British!

I was working for a small (25-person) architectural firm in downtown Boston that was led by our elder president (who was very proper and very British, with a heavy accent). It was the time of year when the company conducted its annual marketing campaign. This was where everyone in the office (including the president) spent three days designing, printing, and physically assembling collateral material to send out to 500+ prospective clients around the country. This effort caused all corners of the office to be in production mode, with everyone assigned a specific task – labeling envelopes, assembling packets, working the postage meter, etc. Mr. Smith's (not his real name) job was to personally sign each cover letter before it was placed in the white manila envelope.

It was an amazing sight to behold. It was a blur of teamwork efficiency.

We were all humming along when, in the middle of this buzz of activity, Mr. Smith decided to walk out of his office to stretch his legs and flex his hand, which we all thought was to relieve the onset of writer's cramp. He casually wandered around the office asking individuals how they were doing. Then Mr. Smith approached one of my co-workers, Mark, who was working beside me, and asked him how things were going.

Without even looking up, and using a spot-on impersonation of a British accent, Mark replied, "All of us are moving along quite well, sir, but we seem to be falling desperately behind in the *signature department!*" The entire office broke out in an uproar of laughter. Mr. Smith returned to his office in a huff while everyone else reached over to give Mark high-fives.

Team Building

At the start of global virtual team meetings, where members come from a variety of cultures, I include a team-building activity of some type. This enables members to get to know each other and build relationships. I ask a member of the team to lead the activity, which is usually a question we want everyone to answer. Nothing elaborate, but it gets people engaged from the start, and it's a fun activity that enables them to get to know each other outside of work. Examples of questions include: Tell us one thing about your culture that's surprising to others. What's one thing that everyone should see or visit if they come to your location? What is your favorite weekend activity? This works!

Miscommunications

As Senior Director of Project Management for a telecom consulting company, I was responsible for managing large, multi-year engineering engagements to build telecommunication networks. On this particular day I was reminded that even an experienced project manager needs to pay attention to the basics.

As the result of a federal grant I was leading a large telecom project expanding an existing, statewide fiber network to bring broadband access to underserved or unserved communities. This can be an extremely challenging undertaking because of the number of geographically dispersed communication channels, including federal, state, county, and city agencies, as well as private land owners, various contractors, and consultants.

On this day, during a routine project status call, the recipient brought to the team's attention a situation that subjected our project to a performance improvement plan issued by the federal funding agency. This, needless to say, is the last thing any project manager or project owner wants to hear on a status call. As a seasoned project manager, I thought I was doing the right things. We held weekly calls with the sub-recipient in which program requirements were reviewed and routes discussed. There were also calls between the cultural consultant and the sub-recipient's construction field manager to relay the exact areas of the project deemed culturally sensitive.

In the end, it was determined that there was a miscommunication between the cultural consultant and the sub-recipient's field manager, which resulted in construction occurring without the required survey (Strike 1!) and without an approved monitor (Strike 2!). When the mistakes were discovered, they weren't relayed through proper channels to the project manager or to the federal program officer (Strike 3!).

This was a very serious communication failure that resulted in the project being placed under an extremely onerous and stringent performance improvement plan. As a direct result of the painful lessons learned in this situation, the team took decisive actions to ensure that it wouldn't happen again. Afterward, we received praise from the federal program officer on our increased communication and related reporting transparency.

These actions helped the project team regain the program's trust. In fact, what started out as a potential project killer uncovered in a status meeting turned into a learning event and a success story for our project. Mistakes will happen on a project, but they don't have to be your project's death knell! Using direct, proactive, and appropriately targeted, resolution-oriented communications – including well planned meetings – can help turn a bad situation into a success if your heart and head are in the right place and the team works together.

Another Bathroom Break

I recall that once we had a kickoff meeting with a major player in the pharma industry. We were a team of three (project leader, business developer, and technical manager); we paid a visit to the customer's site for the kickoff, and it went smoothly during the morning. We had a small lunch break and resumed the meeting afterwards. The meeting room was quiet, with very little noise interference . . . except from my colleague's stomach! He was nervous the whole time because he didn't feel confident with his English, and to make matters worse, lunch didn't sit too well in his tummy. So you an imagine – a lot of persistent intestinal noise. At first everyone pretended to not hear it, until we all cracked up and my colleague excused himself and rushed to the bathroom. It could be seen as an ice-breaker since we laughed so much. Even today we remember it with a big smile on our faces!

Joined at the Hip

The first global workshop that I facilitated was in Munich, Germany, with 20 participants from all across the globe. Early on I could tell that the stakeholders were reluctant to participate. As it turned out, the invitation sent to these stakeholders never mentioned that it was for a project planning workshop! Several of them thought that the purpose of the workshop was to receive and review the output of a planning workshop that had already happened. I wasn't copied on the actual workshop invitation, so I didn't see the potential for problems. The key lesson that I learned was to stay joined at the hip with the assigned project manager prior to and during the workshop so that I would be made aware of any challenges to the success of the workshop.

Going Quite Swimmingly

We had a project meeting with three companies to pre-plan a Manager on Duty (MOD) customer meeting. It was summer and we were staying in a hotel in the southwest of the United Kingdom, and we decided to have the meeting around the swimming pool. This had a very positive impact on reaching triparty agreement on our approach before we met the customer. Was it the chlorine or the stylish swimwear? Don't know for sure, but it worked.

Old School Sometimes Rules

In a planning meeting for an Oracle Financials project we realized that people were looking at different versions of the plan. They hadn't kept up with the numerous changes that resulted from customer change requests. We asked the project administrator to physically collect paper from everyone and to print new copies on the spot to save a lot of misunderstanding. It's good to be green, but sometimes paper makes you more efficient and greener in the long run.

Expand the Band

In one particular meeting, we asked everyone on the main team (other project managers, architects, project office managers) to bring their seconds-in-command to the meeting so that they could see what was going on. As a result, we had a lot more courteous and honest contributions!

It's the Little Things that Count

Little things – even *minute* things – matter. For a complex project we held regular joint meetings with the customers' project management team. Minutes were always taken, but people never agreed to the minutes of the previous meeting. Our breakthrough was to have the last item on the agenda of each meeting be an action to have everyone *agree to the minutes!* It actually helped people's understanding too, because to gain agreement the minute points had to be clearly summarized with everyone present, and no-one could say that they didn't remember agreeing to a minute item. It's the *minute* (pun intended!) things that can make a difference.

One House!

I was facilitating a weekly status meeting when an issue was brought up by one of the software engineers. While he was speaking, the tester started a conversation, a very audible one, with a fellow tester. So now two conversations were going on in my meeting. Then another conversation between developers ensued in response to the first one, drowning out the others. I sat in shock as I lost control of my meeting by trying to listen to all these individuals. Frustrated at the chaos, I screamed, "One house!" The meeting got quiet as the attendees turned and looked at me with a "huh?" look. "One house" was something that was yelled, when I worked on a project in Nigeria, to get everyone's attention. Realizing that they didn't understand what I meant, I said, "One person at a time, please." But I'm sure that it was the One House phrase that got their attention!

Glossary

Agile/Adaptive. A methodology of managing projects that grew out of software development, it's iterative and adaptive, creating deliverables in short (up to one month) iterations or sprints. Self-organizing teams work closely with product owners to continually create business value. It tends to be very change-driven. (Compare with waterfall.) Variants include Scrum, XP, and Lean.

Assumption. For the purposes of project management (and in particular for this book, which is focused on meetings), think of an assumption as the seed of a risk. If you assume, for example, that the price of a key material for your project is steady, and that price triples, then that assumption has germinated and started to grow into a threat. The formal definition of an assumption is something considered to be true without any proof. From a meeting perspective, what's important is to make these assumptions widely known and documented – and to consider them when you're identifying risks.

Baseline. A baseline is a reference, based on original project starting conditions, against which all measurements will be compared. Baselines are approved by key stakeholders. Three baselines – schedule baseline, cost baseline, and scope baseline – are used in project management to look for variance and make changes. The baseline can be changed, but only with formal change control.

Communications plan. A plan that details how communications will flow. For example, there will be a weekly team meeting to discuss action items, schedule, and risks. There will be a monthly steering committee meeting to advise senior management of progress. There will be a lessons learned meeting at the end of each phase to determine what can be done better.

Constraint. A limit that cannot be exceeded. In the case of projects, we're normally talking about budget, schedule, and scope. See *triple constraint*.

Crashing. A form of schedule compression in which extra resources are put on critical-path tasks to get those specific tasks done more quickly. This can potentially bring the project's end date in earlier than indicated by a natural determination of the critical path. It may result in increased risk and/or cost. Adding too many people may lead to the law of diminishing returns.

Critical path. In a network diagram, this is the longest path through the network, which, in turn, defines the shortest time possible in which the project could be completed without applying techniques such as fast-tracking or crashing. A critical-path task will have no slack (float), which means that if it slips, even by one second, that one-second delay will cause the same delay in the end date. There may be more than one critical path in a network. See *network diagram*.

Critical Success Factors (CSFs). When creating critical success factors, remember that they always relate to objectives. Exhibit E.1 shows how our case study may develop critical success factors from its objectives.

Dependency. A dependency is a relationship between tasks in which one must be completed before the other. They are represented by arrows in a network diagram (see Exhibit E.2). In our case study, we cannot put on the candles, for example, until the two dependencies (Obtain Candles and Frost and Decorate Cake) are completed.

Estimate. A forecast regarding how long an activity will take, how many resources might be required, or how much it will cost.

Facilitate. To make it possible or easier for something to happen.

Fast tracking. A form of schedule compression in which you do tasks in parallel that are usually, for best practice reasons, done in sequence (for example, making sure that a design is complete before beginning construction). This tends to increase risk and may also increase costs.

OBJECTIVE	CRITICAL SUCCESS FACTOR	SUCCESS CRITERIA
Gain 25% more of the electorate with the environment as a top concern.	Assemble compelling information about the sustainability elements of this home.	90% of appropriate statistics compiled within 2 months of launch
	Assure that the information is conveyed to the target voters.	50% increase in website hits 75% positive reaction on social media
Maintain a Think Globally, Act Locally way of working in the project.	Group discussion of draft schedule, action items	95% of all workers are from within a 25-mile radius.
Assure that selected vendors are ethical and responsible.	Use intern staff to vet vendors.	100% of vendors vetted
	Review Lessons Learned from similar sustainable housing projects	At least two other similar projects are used for lessons learned.
	Involve vendor stakeholders early in the project to assure their buy-in to objectives and working principles.	85% attendance rate for key identified stakeholders at kickoff
Achieve and document 45% energy reduction after 2 years.	Baseline current energy use.	Baseline complete by 30 March 2019
	Assure that utility service providers are recording ongoing energy use.	100% of providers have committed by 15 July 2019
	Use intern staff to collect, compare, and report data each month for the 24-month period.	Benchmark: Achieve 30% savings within first year.
	Acquire LEED expert for consultation	N/A

Exhibit E.1. Critical success factors are developed from the project's objectives. Here are the CSFs for our sustainable house case study.

Float. The amount of time that a task can slip without delaying the project's end date (see slack).

Gantt chart. The Gantt chart is named in honor of Henry Gantt, an American mechanical engineer and management consultant known for the development of scientific management. It's a visual representation of the WBS with the element of time and a calendar added. The Gantt Chart uses bars to represent when the tasks start and end, arrows to represent

Network Diagram Showing Dependencies

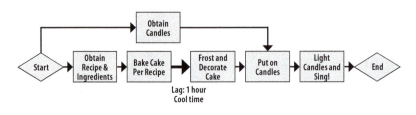

Exhibit E.2. Dependencies are represented by arrows in this network diagram, which shows the critical path (Obtain Candles–Put on Candles–Light Candles and Sing!) for baking a cake.

dependencies, and diamonds to represent milestones. It may also track resource usage, percent compete, and other attributes. Exhibit E.3 shows a simple example using our bake-a-cake saga described in our glossary entry for *network diagram.*

Issue log. Similar to a risk register, but dedicated instead to issues – threats that have already been triggered or are currently occurring. Issue logs are in place to assure that issues have owners and dates for resolution and are tracked to resolution.

Milestone. An important project moment usually representing a key project accomplishment or due date, such as End of 3rd Quarter or Complete Audit or Field Test Complete. Milestones have zero duration by definition and are represented as diamonds on network diagrams and Gantt charts.

Network diagram. A means of displaying the project schedule in terms of project tasks, their durations, and interdependencies. If, for example, you need to know how long it will take to prepare a homemade birthday cake for a party, you need to get ingredients, bake the cake, frost the cake, and decorate the cake. In parallel you could buy candles. Arrows show dependencies and the amount of slack (float) available for each task. It can also indicate any lag times (such as baking time) and lead time (like allowing a task to have a head start).

The network diagram is best for graphically showing the critical path of the project – the sequence of tasks in which a delay of any of them will cause the project to fail to meet its planned end-date. In our highly

Gantt Chart

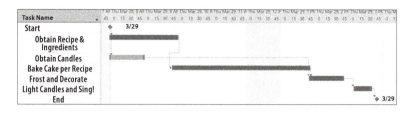

Task Name																											

Exhibit E.3. A sample Gantt chart for baking a cake. A Gantt chart is a visual representation of the WBS with the element of time and a calendar added.

simplified example, if Obtain Candles turns out to be eight hours, it will make the path Obtain Candles–Put on Candles–Light Candles–Sing the longest path (critical path) through the network.

Nominal Group Technique (NGT). *Nominal* means "in name only" – so this is not a functional work group, but a hybrid work group, which is what comprises a project team – so this fits projects very well. NGT is a four-step process to effectively and efficiently generate good ideas or solutions that will come from the project team (CDC 2006). The four steps are: Generating Ideas, Recording Ideas, Discussing Ideas, and Voting On Ideas.

The technique's goal is to reach consensus. NGT does this by asking individuals to respond to questions posed by a facilitator, who asks team members to prioritize the ideas or suggestions of all group members. The process prevents the domination of the discussion by a single person, encourages all group members to participate, and results in a set of prioritized solutions or recommendations that truly represent the group's preferences.

Project charter. The fundamental document that authorizes a project and names the project manager. It's meant to be a terse, concise document that summarizes the objectives, stakeholders, high-level budget, assumptions, and risks.

RACI matrix. This is one form of a responsibility assignment matrix, and it maps the *what* (the tasks of the project) to the *who* (the contributors to the project). RACI stands for responsible, accountable, consulted, and informed, and (see Exhibit 9.1) at the intersection of the *what* and the *who* it defines just what the contributor contributes.

Requirement. A capability needed in a product, service, application, or result that satisfies a need – solving a problem or achieving an objective of a stakeholder. Typically, requirements for projects are from customers or the project team itself. An example of a customer requirement: the software must be able to provide its result on a PC, tablet, or smartphone screen. An example of a project requirement: project team meetings must have an agenda.

Risk register. A list of the risks on the project, including both threats (negative risks) and opportunities (positive risks), that captures the risk, risk type, risk owner, planned risk response, possible secondary or residual risks, and more. From a meeting perspective this is important, since risk should be a conscious agenda item at every other project meeting, at a minimum.

Schedule. Although it may be displayed in many forms, the schedule serves to show how activities in the project take place over time and as well as the linkages between the activities. Some examples of how a project schedule could be conveyed at meetings (and in general) depend on the audience and intent of the communication, and include:

- Using a regular calendar with key project milestones highlighted
- A milestone chart or summary table of key milestone events
- A Gantt chart
- A network diagram (with or without timeline)

In all of the cases, the schedule is focused on the *when* of the project. It's important to note that the scope is determined first, or the schedule won't reflect the full set of project activities and may be missing key dependencies.

Scope. What is *in* and *not in* a project. Scope must not only be clearly defined but must be carefully controlled. Otherwise the project may incrementally and dangerously expand, leading to increased costs and delayed schedule. After all, scope is one side of the classic triple constraint of project management. The main component of scope is the work focused on the project's outcome. However, it's important to understand that this has two components – *project scope* and *product scope*. Project scope is the work performed on behalf of the delivery of the project's product, service, or result. For example, if we're building a home, and we discover that having nourishing snacks for the construction workers makes a big difference in their productivity, we may choose to provide those snacks. The snacks themselves are not delivered to the homeowners, but they are important and are a part of *project* scope. *Product* scope, in this example, would include the home itself as well as landscaping, installation of appliances, whatever was defined as the final deliverable(s), and delivered to customers.

Slack. Also called float or total float, this is the amount of time a task can slip without delaying the end date of the project. A critical path will, by definition, have zero float.

Stakeholder. A person or organization that is affected by your project or the project's outcome. If you're building a bridge, the stakeholders would be the construction workers, the project team members, the suppliers of materials, the pedestrians and drivers who use the bridge, the businesses whose sales may change based on changed traffic patterns . . . as you can see, a stakeholder has a broad definition. It's imperative that you do a broad and deep identification of stakeholders because stakeholders bring with them their own set of risks – both threats and opportunities. The project manager has to balance the competing objectives of stakeholders.

Triple constraint. This is a way to think of the three most important and interdependent constraints that all projects face – time (schedule), cost (budget), and scope (what's in and not in the project). Typically you cannot change one of the constraints without affecting either one or both of the other constraints. Be sure that your project team is aware not only of this concept but also of the priority of each of these in your particular project. Make that prioritization a recurring theme at your meetings.

Waterfall. A methodology that defines the project life cycle as a series of phases that must be completed before moving on to the next one (see Exhibit E.4). Phases can be run in an overlapping or parallel fashion at the expense of some risk. Waterfall tends to be very plan-driven. See *agile/adaptive*.

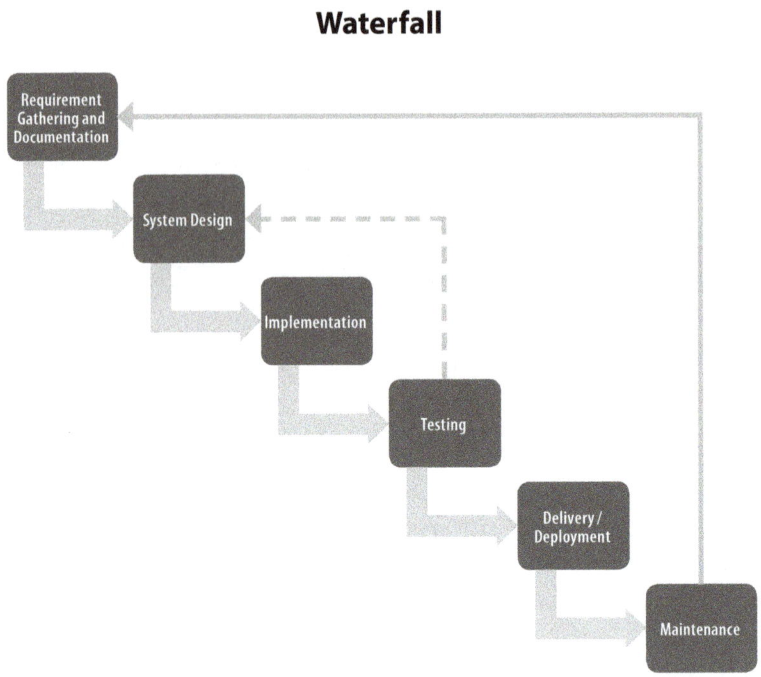

Waterfall

Exhibit E.4. Waterfall is a methodology that defines the project life cycle as a series of phases that must be completed before moving on to the next phase. The dotted line represents possible iterations based on the results of testing.

Work Breakdown Structure (WBS). A hierarchical structure to visualize the scope of a project. Think of it as an organization chart for your project. It's important to remember that the WBS depicts everything that's in your project, including both product scope (the features and deliverables of your product) as well as project scope (aspects needed to deliver that product scope). The WBS's lower levels will show work packages that can be assigned to individual groups or organizations and can also be used for accounting purposes (charging hours), and that will form the basis of the tasks on the Gantt chart. The sum of all of the elements in the WBS must represent *everything* that's needed to deliver the project's outcome (which will be at the very top of the WBS). A partial WBS is shown in Exhibit 9.4 to give you the idea. Foundation, Frame, etc. would be broken down similar to the way that Electrical and Solar Roof are as shown in the illustration.

APPENDIX F

Project Templates

W E'VE MADE AVAILABLE SEVERAL TEMPLATES for you. Download them at projectmeetings.us or mavenhousepress.com/our-books/ project-meetings/. The templates include the following:

- Communications Matrix
- Issues and Actions Log
- RACI Matrix
- Risk Register
- Stakeholder Register
- Team Planning Readiness Checklist

REFERENCES

Alexander, Moira. 2015. "Planning is Key to Project Management Success." *CIO*, June 10. Accessed May 1, 2018, https://www.cio.com/article/2932987/project-management/planning-is-key-to-project-management-success.html.

Anderson, Erika. 2014. "Why Most Meetings Are Awful and What You Can Do About It." *Forbes*, January 22. Accessed May 1, 2018, https://www.forbes.com/sites/erikaandersen/2014/01/22/why-most-meetings-are-awful-and-what-you-can-do-about-it/#1c8afbf1649a.

Axtel, Paul. 2015. "The Right Way to End a Meeting." *Harvard Business Review*, March 11. Accessed May 5, 2018, https://hbr.org/2015/03/the-right-way-to-end-a-meeting.

Basu, Shankha, and Krishna Savani. 2017. "To Make Better Choices, Look at All Your Options Together." *Harvard Business Review*, June 28. Accessed May 12, 2018, https://hbr.org/2017/06/to-make-better-choices-look-at-all-your-options-together?utm_campaign=hbr&utm_source=twitter&utm_medium=social.

Butchtik, Liliana. 2010. *Secrets to Mastering the WBS in Real-World Projects*. Newtown Square, PA: Project Management Institute.

Caetano, Taina, Paulo Caroli, and Glauber Ramos. 2016. *Fun Retrospectives: Activities and Ideas for Making Agile Retrospectives More Engaging*. British Columbia: LeanPub.

CDC. 2006. "Gaining Consensus Among Stakeholders Through the Nominal Group Technique." Department of Health and Human Services Evaluation Briefs, November. Accessed May 10, 2018, https://www.cdc.gov/healthyyouth/evaluation/pdf/brief7.pdf.

Crowe, Andy. 2016. *Alpha Project Managers: What The Top 2% Know That Everyone Else Does Not*. Kennesaw, GA: Velociteach.

Duggal, Jack S. (2012). "Managing the DANCE: Think Design, Not Plan. Paper presented at PMI° Global Congress 2012 – North America, Vancouver, Canada. Newtown Square, PA: Project Management Institute. Accessed May 1, 2018, http://www.pmi.org/learning/ library/dance-complex-project-design-framework-reality-6094.

Economy, Peter. 2016. "7 Ways to End Every Meeting on a Positive Note." *Inc.*, May 19. Accessed May 5, 2018, https://www.inc.com/ peter-economy/7-effortless-ways-to-end-every-meeting-on-a-positive-note.html.

Goman, Carol Kinsey. 2015. "How The Best Salespeople Read Body Language." *Forbes*, December 1. Accessed May 12, 2018, https:// www.forbes.com/sites/carolkinseygoman/2015/12/01/why-the-best-salespeople-read-body-language/2/#4b5335dc1774.

Hancock, Andrienne B., and Benjamin A. Rubin. 2014. "Influence of Communication Partner's Gender on Language." *Journal of Language and Social Psychology*, May 11.

Hastie, Shane, and Stéphane Wojewoda. 2015. "Standish Group 2015 Chaos Report – Q&A with Jennifer Lynch." InfoQ, October 4. Accessed May 10, 2018, https://www.infoq.com/articles/standish-chaos-2015.

Hofstede Insights. 2018a. "Country Culture Tools." Accessed May 11, 2018, https://www.hofstede-insights.com/country-culture-tools/.

Hofstede Insights. 2018b. "Organisational Culture." Accessed May 11, 2018, www.hofstede-insights.com/models/organisational-culture/.

Hofstede Insights. 2018c. "The 6 Dimensions of National Culture." Accessed May 11, 2018,https://www.hofstede-insights.com/ models/national-culture/.

Hubbard, Douglas W. 2014. *How to Measure Anything*. New York: Wiley.

IHG. 2013. "Global Research Report Finds that Companies Could Increase Revenue by Investing in More Face-to-Face Meetings." InterContinental Hotels Group. Accessed May 12, 2018, https:// www.ihgplc.com/en/news-and-media/news-releases/2013/ face-facts--global-research-report-finds-that-companies-could-increase-revenue-by-investing-in-more.

Jensen, Keld. 2014. "Are Physical Meetings Becoming Outdated: Could Saving $10,000 Cost You $1M?" *Forbes*, August 21. Accessed May 5, 2018, https://www.forbes.com/sites/keldjensen/2014/08/21/are-physical-meetings-becoming-outdated-could-saving-10000-cost-you-1000000/#6de130e366ca.

Kilmann, Ralph H. 2018. "An Overview of the Thomas-Kilmann Conflict Mode Instrument (TKI)." Kilmann Diagnostics. Accessed May 5, 2018, http://www.kilmanndiagnostics.com/overview-thomas-kilmann-conflict-mode-instrument-tki.

Lennox, Abbie. 2013. "The Importance of Face-to-Face Meetings." Your Coffee Break, November 20. Accessed May 12, 2018, http://www.yourcoffeebreak.co.uk/career-guide/26338738995/the-importance-of-face-to-face-meetings/.

Nazlieva, Nesrin. 2018. "The Dos and Don'ts of Dealing with Dutch Colleagues." Together Abroad, Accessed May 11, 2008, https://www.togetherabroad.nl/page/blog/command/detail/uid/8nf2vg/3/bb/1/the-do-s-and-don-ts-of-dealing-with-dutch-colleagues.

Nilsen, Ella. 2018. "The Bipartisan Group Behind Sen. Susan Collins's "Talking Stick," Explained." Vox.com, January 23. Accessed May 1, 2018, https://www.vox.com/policy-and-politics/2018/1/23/16920060/susan-collins-talking-stick-senate-bipartisan-government-shutdown.

Project Management Institute. 2017. *A Guide to the Project Management Body of Knowledge (PMBOK® Guide), Sixth Edition.* Newtown Square, PA: Project Management Institute.

Scaled Agile. 2018. "Agile Release Train." SAFe. Accessed June 14, 2018, https://www.scaledagileframework.com/agile-release-train/

Schwaber, Ken, and Jeff Sullivan. 2017. *The Scrum Guide.* Ken Schwaber and Jeff Sullivan. Accessed May 5, 2018, https://www.scrum.org/resources/scrum-guide.

Searcy, Tom. 2012. "Meetings Suck, Make Them Better." *Inc.*, May 29. Accessed May 1, 2018, https://www.inc.com/tom-searcy/meetings-suck-make-them-better.html?nav=next.

Serrador, Pedro. 2012. "The Importance of the Planning Phase to Project Success." Paper presented at PMI° Global Congress 2012 – North America, Vancouver, British Columbia, Canada. Newtown Square, PA: Project Management Institute. Accessed May 1, 2018, https://www.pmi.org/learning/library/importance-planning-phase-project-success-6021.

Strobbe, Marieke, Hans Veenman, Leo de Bruijn, and Menno Valkenburg. 2017. *Five Frustrations of Project Managers.* Amsterdam: Mediawerf Uitgevers.

Sustainable Buildings Industry Council. 2016. "Green Principles for Residential Design." *Whole Building Design Guide*, August 5. Accessed May 1, 2018, https://www.wbdg.org/resources/green-principles-residential-design.

Tuckman, Bruce. 1965. "Developmental Sequence in Small Groups." *Psychological Bulletin* 63 (6): 384–99.

Valdesolo, Piercarlo. 2013. "Psychologists Uncover Hidden Signals of Trust – Using a Robot." *Scientific American*, January 8. Accessed May 1, 2018, https://www.scientificamerican.com/article/psychologist-uncover-hidden-signals-of-trust-using-a-robot/.

Zimmerman, Donald, and Candace West. 1996. "Sex Roles, Interruptions, and Silences in Conversation." In *Towards a Critical Sociolinguistics* edited by Rajendra Singh. Amsterdam: John Benjamins Publishing Company.

Zucker, Allen. 2016. "Successful Projects: What We Really Know." Project Management Essentials, October 1. Accessed May 1, 2018, https://pmessentials.us/successful-projects-really-know/.

INDEX

ABOUT THE AUTHORS

Rich Maltzman, PMP

An engineer since 1978, and a project management supervisor since 1988, Rich's project work has been diverse, including the integration of the program management offices (PMOs) of two large merging corporations. Rich has also consulted and taught at several universities in the United States and China. He has co-authored several books, including the Cleland Award Winner *Green Project Management* and has developed project management professional (PMP) exam prep courseware, including exams and books. Rich has presented at international PMI and IPMA conferences throughout the world. Rich holds a BSEE from the UMass Amherst, an MSIE from Purdue, a mini-MBA from the University of Pennsylvania's Wharton School, and a master's certificate in international business management from Indiana University's Kelley School of Business/INSEAD.

Jim Stewart, PMP, CSM

With over twenty-five years of experience, Jim has managed numerous multi-million-dollar international IT programs. He spearheaded the implementation of a $20 million Virtual Private Network for a major telecommunications company and managed the international deployment of a transaction system for IBM partners. Since 2003, as a principal of JP Stewart Associates, Jim has been engaged in consulting, training, and mentoring for organizations. A PMP since 2001 and Certified Scrum Master (CSM) since 2013, he helps organizations incorporate best practices and has set up several project management offices. Jim has taught at Brandeis, UMass Boston, Bentley, and Northeastern, is a frequent speaker at PMI gatherings and is on the advisory board at the e-learning company MindEdge, Inc. Jim holds a BA from Boston University.

Wayne Turmel

Wayne is a writer, speaker, and entrepreneur and cofounder of the Remote Leadership Institute. He's the author of six non-fiction books, including *Meet Like You Mean It: A Leader's Guide to Painless and Productive Virtual Meetings*.

Teresa Lawrence, PhD, PMP, CSM

Teresa is president of International Deliverables, LLC. She's a creator, integrator, and implementer of creativity/creative problem solving into project management across all industries and methodologies.

CPSIA information can be obtained
at www.ICGtesting.com
Printed in the USA
LVHW050952120219
607255LV00006B/15/P

9 781938 548260